Digital Nomad

How to Become a Digital Nomad

(Master the Art of Remote Work and Secure a Location-independent Income)

David Maciel

Published By **Gautam Kumar**

David Maciel

All Rights Reserved

Digital Nomad: How to Become a Digital Nomad (Master the Art of Remote Work and Secure a Location-independent Income)

ISBN 978-1-7781779-9-6

No part of this guidebook shall be reproduced in any form without permission in writing from the publisher except in the case of brief quotations embodied in critical articles or reviews.

Legal & Disclaimer

The information contained in this book is not designed to replace or take the place of any form of medicine or professional medical advice. The information in this book has been provided for educational & entertainment purposes only.

The information contained in this book has been compiled from sources deemed reliable, and it is accurate to the best of the Author's knowledge; however, the Author cannot guarantee its accuracy and validity and cannot be held liable for any errors or omissions. Changes are periodically made to this book. You must consult your doctor or get professional medical advice before using any of the suggested remedies, techniques, or information in this book.

Upon using the information contained in this book, you agree to hold harmless the Author from and against any damages, costs, and expenses, including any legal fees potentially resulting from the application of any of the information provided by this guide. This disclaimer applies to any damages or injury caused by the use and application, whether directly or indirectly, of any advice or information presented, whether for breach of contract, tort, negligence, personal injury, criminal intent, or under any other cause of action.

You agree to accept all risks of using the information presented inside this book. You need to consult a professional medical practitioner in order to ensure you are both able and healthy enough to participate in this program.

Table Of Contents

Chapter 1: Preparing For the Digital Nomad Lifestyle 1

Chapter 2: Setting Up Your Digital Nomad Office 13

Chapter 3: Managing Finances as a Digital Nomad 25

Chapter 4: Finding Accommodation and Transportation 39

Chapter 5: Embracing the Local Culture and Language 52

Chapter 6: Staying Healthy and Balanced As a Digital Nomad 67

Chapter 7: Overcoming Common Digital Nomad Challenges 81

Chapter 8: Building a Sustainable Digital Nomad Career 97

Chapter 9: Repatriation and Transitioning 112

Chapter 10: Attractions of Living a Nomadic Life 121

Chapter 11: Managing Finances and Budgeting As a Nomad 132

Chapter 12: Navigating Cultural Shifts .. 143

Chapter 13: Accessing Medical Services and Healthcare Abroad 149

Chapter 14: Historical Evolution of Remote Work 161

Chapter 15: Tips for Continuous Learning and Improvement 176

Chapter 1: Preparing For The Digital Nomad Lifestyle

Assessing Your Skills and Finding

As a virtual nomad, the liberty to art work and stay anywhere within the worldwide is one of the maximum appealing additives of this manner of lifestyles. However, earlier than you embark in this exciting adventure, it's miles essential to evaluate your skills and discover far flung paintings opportunities that align together together with your understanding. This subchapter wills manual expats, folks who want to artwork distant places, and those who aspire to stay and artwork out of the country in figuring out their skills and exploring diverse avenues for far off work.

"Travel takes us out of our comfort zones and evokes us to appearance, flavor

and attempt new subjects."

Firstly, take the time to evaluate your current capabilities and decide how they may be translated into a miles flung paintings placing. Consider your professional historical past, schooling, and any specialized information you personal. Are you a skilled writer, picture designer, programmer, or marketer? Are you informed in a specific issue or company? Identifying your middle skills will help you understand the form of a long way off paintings possibilities which may be most suitable for you.

Next, studies the unique digital nomad niches that exist in current international interest marketplace. From freelance writing and digital help to software software development and on line tutoring, there may be a big style of some distance flung art work alternatives to be had. Explore these niches and spot which align collectively along with your skills and pastimes. Additionally, recall the decision for and market inclinations within each niche to make sure you pick out

out a region that gives sufficient opportunities for some distance flung paintings.

Networking is critical even as on the lookout for a ways flung paintings possibilities. Join virtual nomad businesses, attend industry meetings, and hook up with professionals on your selected challenge. These connections can bring about activity referrals, collaborations, and treasured insights into the far off paintings panorama. Social media systems like LinkedIn and on-line activity boards devoted to some distance flung work also can characteristic valuable resources for locating machine opportunities.

Furthermore, it is essential to create a compelling online presence that showcases your abilties and knowledge. Develop a expert net internet site or portfolio that highlights your preceding paintings and demonstrates your capabilities. Utilize social media structures to percent your expertise and engage with organisation experts. This online presence will no longer excellent attraction to ability customers or employers but moreover set up your credibility as a much flung worker.

Lastly, continuously replace and beautify your abilities to stay competitive in the far off paintings market. Take on-line guides, attend webinars, and live informed approximately the modern-day day enterprise trends. This dedication to expert improvement will open doorways to greater some distance flung paintings opportunities and help you thrive as a virtual nomad.

In conclusion, assessing your capabilities and locating some distance off artwork opportunities is a crucial step in becoming a a hit virtual nomad. By information your strengths, exploring severa niches, networking, constructing an internet presence, and constantly improving your abilities, you can embark on an thrilling adventure of jogging and dwelling anywhere in the global..

Creating a Financial Plan

One of the important thing factors of effectively becoming a digital nomad is growing a robust financial plan. As an expat or someone who wants to art work and stay remote places, it's far critical to have a clean information of your fee range and the manner you can maintain your way of life at the same time as being region independent. In this financial disaster, we are able to discover the crucial steps to create a economic plan as a way to help your digital nomad adventure.

1. Assess your present day economic scenario: Before embarking on your digital nomad adventure, it's important to evaluate your cutting-edge financial reputation.

Take stock of your earnings, costs, money owed, and financial financial savings. This assessment will help you determine how an lousy lot you want to hold or earn to hold your preferred lifestyle remote places.

2. Define your financial dreams: Set smooth monetary desires that align together together along with your virtual nomad aspirations. Do

you want to shop a selected quantity every month? Are you aiming to emerge as debt-unfastened? Understanding your goals will help you create a roadmap for task them.

three. Budgeting: Establishing a price range is essential for handling your fee range efficaciously. Take into attention your predicted earnings and allocate charge range for necessities together with accommodation, transportation, food, healthcare, and enjoyment. Consider the charge of residing in your preferred destination, and be sensible about your spending conduct.

4. Establish an emergency fund: As a digital nomad, it's crucial to have a safety net for surprising fees or durations of low profits. Set aside a part of your earnings each month into an emergency fund that may cowl at least three to six months of residing costs.

5. Explore multiple income streams: To make certain financial balance, it is useful to have a couple of income streams as a digital nomad. Besides your number one supply of earnings,

maintain in thoughts freelancing, some distance off art work contracts, online groups, or investments that could generate additional sales.

6. Manage taxes and crook obligations: Research the tax necessities and jail responsibilities in every your home u . S . And your vacation spot. Understand how being a virtual nomad may have an impact on your tax liability and ensure compliance with close by hints.

7. Seek expert recommendation: If you are uncertain about dealing with your rate range as a digital nomad, bear in mind consulting economic advisors who cognizance on expat or global finance. They can provide precious insights and assist you optimize your economic plan.

Remember, growing a monetary plan is an ongoing device. Regularly assessment and adjust your finances, economic financial financial savings, and investments to ensure they align along with your evolving manner of existence and goals. By taking these steps, you will be properly-organized to navigate the financial elements of your digital nomad adventure and revel in the freedom and versatility of operating and living everywhere in the international.

Choosing Your Destination

One of the most thrilling components of being a virtual nomad is the freedom to choose out your very private excursion spot.

As a digital nomad, you have got had been given an appropriate possibility to artwork and live everywhere in the worldwide. However, this freedom can also be overwhelming, particularly in case you're new to the digital nomad manner of existence. That's why it is critical to carefully recall and select your vacation spot earlier than embarking on your virtual nomad adventure.

When it involves deciding on your tour spot, there are various elements to recollect. First and predominant, keep in mind the kind of lifestyle you want to influence. Are you a town individual, or do you make a decision on the tranquility of nature?

Do you experience a bustling nightlife or pick out out a extra laid-once more surroundings? Consider your non-public options and select out a destination that aligns along with your favored manner of life.

Another important trouble to remember is the value of dwelling in your preferred tour spot. As a virtual nomad, you could need to make sure that your income can cover your charges. Research the rate of lodging, transportation, meals, and special essentials to your desired place. This will assist making a decision whether or not it's far a financially feasible preference for you.

Additionally, it is crucial to take into account the infrastructure and facilities to be had in your preferred holiday spot. Check the supply and satisfactory of internet connections, as a strong and rapid net connection is crucial for a long way flung work. Look into coworking areas or cafes that cater to virtual nomads, as they might offer a supportive operating environment and opportunities to hook up with like-minded human beings..

Furthermore, undergo in mind the local lifestyle, language, and visa necessities of your chosen holiday spot.

Familiarize your self with the neighborhood customs and traditions, as this could help you combine into the local community and make your live extra amusing.

Research the visa requirements and ensure that you have the essential documentation to legally paintings and stay in your selected excursion spot.

Lastly, are seeking out hints and recommendation from fellow digital nomads or expats who've lived to your selected region. Their evaluations and insights can offer precious facts and assist you're making an informed choice..

Remember, choosing your vacation spot is a non-public choice, and what works for one digital nomad might not work for some other. Take the time to assess your alternatives, bear in mind your priorities, and select out out a vacation spot that aligns collectively together with your way of lifestyles and goals.

With careful making plans and studies, you could discover the correct vacation spot to live and paintings as a digital nomad, and embark on a satisfying and rewarding adventure.

Researching Visa Requirements

and Legalities

When embarking on a journey to artwork and live anywhere in the international as a digital nomad, one of the most crucial factors to keep in thoughts is knowing the visa requirements and legalities of your selected excursion spot. Navigating the complex global of visas may be overwhelming, however with the right expertise and studies, you could make certain a easy transition to your new home.

Before diving into the specifics, it's miles critical to recognize that visa necessities variety from u.S. To u . S . A .. Depending on your nationality, the cause of your live, and the length, you can need to use for considered one of a kind sorts of visas, which encompass tourist visas, paintings visas, industrial company visas, or perhaps residency allows.

The first step is to determine the kind of visa that aligns collectively with your goals and intentions..

Chapter 2: Setting Up Your Digital Nomad Office

Essential Tools and Equipment for

Working Remotely

In ultra-current-day virtual age, the idea of labor has advanced drastically. The upward thrust of generation has empowered people to artwork from everywhere in the worldwide, giving transport to a present day-day breed of professionals referred to as digital nomads. For expats, folks that need to paintings overseas, and those which means to live and artwork in a foreign country, the freedom and flexibility offered through a ways flung paintings can be really freeing.

To embark on this interesting journey as a digital nomad, it's far critical to equip yourself with the proper gear and machine at the manner to allow you to work seamlessly from any vicinity. Here are a few important gadgets that every aspiring digital nomad need to hold in mind:

1. Reliable Laptop: Your computer is your lifeline as a digital nomad. Invest in a awesome, mild-weight computer with a long battery existence and sufficient garage capacity to cope with your paintings-associated files and software software program.

2. Stable Internet Connection: A strong and speedy internet connection is the backbone of a ways off paintings.

Research the outstanding internet company vendors in the u . S . You would like to live in and ensure you've got got got a dependable connection to live related with customers and friends.

three. Noise-Canceling Headphones: Working remotely regularly technique working in various environments, along facet bustling cafes or shared workspaces. Noise-canceling headphones can drown out distractions, permitting you to recognition for your responsibilities and hold productiveness.

4. Portable Charger: When jogging at the pass, having a portable charger is critical to keep your gadgets powered up. Invest in a excessive-capability power economic group that could price your computer, cell phone, and awesome devices.

five. Virtual Private Network (VPN): A VPN is vital for keeping on line safety and privacy whilst running remotely. It encrypts your internet connection, defensive sensitive data from functionality cyber threats.

6. Ergonomic Accessories: As a virtual nomad, you could discover yourself strolling prolonged hours. Invest in an ergonomic keyboard, mouse, and chair to maintain right posture and prevent pain and stress.

7. Cloud Storage: Utilize cloud storage offerings along with Dropbox or Google Drive to securely preserve and get right of entry to your files from any device. This guarantees that your artwork is commonly available and sponsored up in case of any sudden situations.

These are only a few critical machine and machine for virtual nomads. Depending for your particular artwork requirements, you can furthermore want greater software utility, verbal exchange device, or specialised tool. As a digital nomad, adaptability is fundamental, so be open to exploring new equipment and technologies which could beautify your faraway art work enjoy.

Remember, being a virtual nomad gives superb possibilities to live and artwork everywhere inside the worldwide.

By equipping your self with the proper gadget and tool, you could revel in the freedom and flexibility that this life-style offers, even as however being capable of supply great work and maintain a a fulfillment career.

Finding Reliable Internet Connections As a digital nomad, having a dependable internet connection is vital on your success and productivity.

Whether you're an expat, someone seeking to artwork remote places, or genuinely want to live and artwork overseas, finding a robust and rapid internet connection is critical for keeping your on line industrial agency or remote interest.

When choosing your vacation spot, it's miles critical to research the great and availability of net connections in that unique u . S . A . Or town. Some international locations may additionally additionally have restricted infrastructure or unreliable net organizations, that can appreciably effect your functionality to paintings efficiently.

One of the first steps to locating a reliable internet connection is to hold in thoughts the sort of accommodations you'll be staying in. Some motels, hostels, or rental houses can also additionally offer complimentary Wi-Fi, but the super and velocity can variety. It is honestly beneficial to have a look at evaluations or achieve out to awesome virtual nomads in on line companies to accumulate records approximately the net reliability in precise motels.

If you rely cautiously on a sturdy internet connection, it can be well really worth making an investment in a portable Wi-Fi device or a close-by SIM card with a facts plan. These options will let you have net get right of entry to wherever you move, presenting you with the energy to paintings from numerous places with out relying on public Wi-Fi networks. Research the nearby telecom agencies on your excursion spot and evaluate their coverage and information plans to discover the top notch opportunity for your dreams.

Another desire to make certain a dependable internet connection is to join a co-jogging vicinity. These areas are particularly designed for a ways off humans and digital nomads, providing excessive-velocity net, comfortable workspaces, and a network of like-minded individuals. Co-walking areas often require a membership price, but the benefits of a dependable connection and a supportive paintings environment can far outweigh the rate.

Lastly, it's miles important to have a backup plan in case of internet outages or disruptions. This can consist of getting offline art work or projects that you may popularity on in the course of downtime, or keeping a list of close by cafes or libraries with dependable Wi-Fi as possibility workspaces.

In quit, locating a reliable net connection is crucial for virtual nomads looking to artwork and stay everywhere in the worldwide. By assignment thorough studies on the net infrastructure of your holiday spot, thinking about portable Wi-Fi devices or nearby information plans, joining co-walking areas, and having backup options, you could make certain which you have a strong and fast internet connection anyplace your travels take you.

Creating a Productive Workspace

As a virtual nomad, your capacity to paintings correctly and successfully is right away tied to the splendid of your workspace. Whether you're running from a cushty café, a shared coworking area, or the comfort of your property, developing a powerful workspace is crucial for maximizing your productiveness and undertaking fulfillment as a digital nomad.

First and number one, it is essential to pick out a workspace that fits your individual needs. Consider elements which include noise stage, lighting, and the deliver of facilities like immoderate-speed internet. Each person has particular possibilities near their artwork environment, so make an effort to check and discover what works exceptional for you.

Keeping your workspace prepared is some different key detail in growing a powerful surroundings. A cluttered workspace can cause distractions and a loss of interest. Invest in storage answers together with record organizers, drawers, and shelves to maintain your workspace tidy and unfastened from useless clutter.

Additionally, make it a dependancy to regularly declutter and dispose of objects which can be no longer needed.

Ergonomics is regularly left out however performs a tremendous function in your typical productivity and physical properly-being. Invest in a cushty chair and a table this is on the right pinnacle on your posture. Consider using a status table or a computer stand to keep away from prolonged sitting, that may result in health problems. Take breaks, stretch, and float round to preserve proper blood flow into and save you fatigue..

Another crucial element of creating a efficient workspace is coping with your digital distractions. The virtual worldwide gives a plethora of distractions, from social media notifications to infinite emails. Set barriers and set up unique instances for checking emails and engaging in social media. Utilize productiveness equipment which incorporates net internet site blockers and time management apps to preserve yourself centered and reduce distractions sooner or later of your art work hours.

Lastly, customize your workspace to make it a location you revel in spending time in. Add flora, artwork, or non-public mementos that encourage and encourage you.

Surrounding your self with things that deliver you pride can extensively beautify your creativity and regular temper.

Remember, your workspace isn't simplest a bodily vicinity, but moreover a intellectual and emotional space. By developing a inexperienced workspace that caters on your desires, you can discover your self induced, centered, and prepared to conquer any artwork challenges that come your way as a virtual nomad.

Whether you're an expat, someone who desires to art work distant places, or in truth a person who wants to stay and artwork in a foreign country, those tips will help you optimize your workspace and maximize your productivity as a virtual nomad.

Managing Your Time and Staying Focused

As a digital nomad, in fact one of the maximum important traumatic conditions you can face is managing some time efficaciously and staying focused while working remotely. The freedom and flexibility that incorporates this way of life can be each a blessing and a curse. Without right challenge and employer, it is smooth to fall into the lure of procrastination and distraction. Here are a few suggestions and strategies that will help you optimize it slow and maintain productiveness as a virtual nomad.

1. Set Clear Goals: Start every day via setting easy, workable desires. Prioritize your responsibilities and spoil them down into smaller, feasible chunks. This will assist you

live targeted and stimulated inside the course of the day.

2. Establish a Routine: While the attraction of being a digital nomad lies within the freedom to paintings from anywhere, it is essential to installation a steady recurring.

Set unique operating hours and create a devoted workspace that is loose from distractions.

3. Minimize Distractions: Distractions can be a productiveness killer. Identify what distracts you the most and take steps to decrease or eliminate them. This must suggest turning off notifications to your cellular phone, the usage of internet net web page-blocking off apps, or locating a quiet coworking area.

four. Time Blocking: Use the technique of time blocking off to allocate unique time slots for one-of-a-type obligations. This will assist you live on the proper tune and prevent multitasking, which can result in reduced productiveness.

Chapter 3: Managing Finances As A Digital Nomad

Handling Taxes and Financial

Obligations

For digital nomads and people residing and working distant places, expertise and efficiently handling taxes and economic duties is important. This subchapter will offer treasured insights and techniques to assist expats, aspiring worldwide people, and virtual nomads navigate the complex international of worldwide taxation and economic duties.

1. Understanding Tax Residency: The first step in dealing with your taxes as a virtual nomad is figuring out your tax residency reputation. We will speak the factors that have an impact on tax residency and provide steerage at the way to installation and maintain tax residency in your private home u . S . A . Or a cutting-edge excursion spot.

2. Global Tax Compliance: As a digital nomad, you may have tax duties in a couple of

worldwide locations. We will discover the concept of double taxation and feature a take a look at techniques to decrease the effect of taxes thru using tax treaties, overseas tax credit score rating, and tax making plans strategies.

3. Choosing the Right Tax Structure: Selecting the right tax form might also have large implications in your economic properly-being. We will speak severa tax systems which incorporates being self-hired, forming a restricted prison duty organization, or strolling as a freelancer and spotlight the pros and cons of every opportunity.

"Not all people who wander are out of place."

four. Digital Nomad-Friendly Countries: Certain international locations offer favorable tax policies and incentives for virtual nomads. We will provide an overview of well-known locations that include virtual nomadism and provide tax benefits, which includes low or no earnings tax, unique visa applications, and tax-super pointers for a ways flung people.

5. Financial Planning and Retirement: Planning on your monetary future is crucial, regardless of your vicinity.

We will delve into strategies for retirement planning, funding management, and wealth safety, ensuring that your international manner of lifestyles would no longer keep away from your prolonged-term economic goals..

6. Navigating Local Regulations: Different nations have unique monetary recommendations and reporting necessities. We will manual you thru the method of statistics and complying with nearby tax criminal pointers, together with submitting tax returns, acquiring vital permits, and staying up to date with changing guidelines.

"Travel is greater than the seeing of points of interest; it's far a trade this is taking place,

deep and permanent, in the thoughts of

dwelling."

7. Working with Tax Professionals: To navigate the complexities of worldwide taxation efficiently, it is frequently useful to are seeking out professional help. We will offer steering on locating in a role tax advisors who focus on serving digital nomads and expats, making sure you obtain correct and tailor-made recommendation.

By mastering the intricacies of taxes and monetary duties, you can with a piece of appropriate fortune encompass the virtual nomad way of existence at the same time as preserving compliance with the legal guidelines of your property u.S. And host worldwide places. With the understanding and strategies supplied in this subchapter, you could create a robust basis for economic success and revel in the liberty and flexibility that contains operating and dwelling anywhere within the global.

Setting Up International Bank Accounts

and Managing Currencies

In brand new interconnected international, the capacity to art work and live everywhere isn't always a miles off dream however a reality for loads. As a virtual nomad, you have the freedom to discover specific global places, revel in numerous cultures, and work remotely. However, handling your fee range while residing remote places may be a daunting project. This subchapter goals to guide expats, those who want to artwork overseas, and those proceeding to live and paintings in another country, in particular digital nomads, on installing international monetary organization money owed and effectively coping with currencies.

Once you have were given were given set up your global financial group account, it is important to amplify effective techniques for managing currencies. Fluctuating change costs can substantially effect your profits and fees. Consider the usage of currency trading apps or net websites to display expenses and make informed choices regarding whilst and in which to alternate currencies. Additionally, discover options for hedging in opposition to overseas money fluctuations, collectively with forward contracts or foreign money futures, to guard your earnings from volatility.

To optimize your remote places cash control, bear in mind diversifying your profits streams. Relying totally on one forex may be risky, specifically if that foreign money is unstable or problem to economic uncertainties. Explore opportunities for freelance paintings or some distance off jobs that pay in awesome currencies. This not great permits to diversify your earnings but moreover offers you with a hedge closer to overseas money risks.

Furthermore, have in thoughts of transaction costs and forex costs at the same time as the usage of your international financial institution account or credit score score gambling cards. These charges can rapid add up and consume into your profits. Look for economic institutions that offer low or no remote places transaction prices, and preserve in mind using on-line charge systems like PayPal or TransferWise for worldwide transfers, as they regularly offer competitive rates and lower expenses.

In end, putting in international economic organization payments and efficiently dealing with currencies are vital skills for virtual nomads and every person living and strolling foreign places. By taking the time to analyze and pick the right international bank, tracking change fees, diversifying earnings streams, and minimizing transaction fees, you could make certain that your financial journey as a virtual nomad is straightforward and a hit.

Budgeting and Cost of Living Considerations

Living and walking overseas as a virtual nomad can be an exciting and worthwhile revel in. However, it is important to consider the financial additives in advance than embarking on this adventure. In this subchapter, we are capable of discover budgeting and charge of residing problems that will help you make informed options and efficaciously manipulate your rate range as a digital nomad.

One of the primary assets you need to do at the same time as planning to stay and paintings out of the country is to create a price range.

This will help you decide how a wonderful deal cash you need to cowl your charges and the way to allocate your price range because it should be. Start with the resource of manner of coming across the charge of residing in the vacation spot united states of america of the usa, which include lodging, transportation, food, healthcare, and distinct important costs.

Compare those prices on your cutting-edge prices to get an idea of the changes you'll want to make.

Another essential interest is knowing the local forex and exchange expenses. Fluctuations in trade charges can substantially impact your finances, so it's miles crucial to display them and plan consequently.

You may also moreover furthermore want to take into account beginning a network financial institution account to keep away from excessive transaction charges and forex expenses.

When it entails lodging, there are various options available to virtual nomads. Renting an condo or residence can often be more charge-effective than staying in inns or short-time period rentals. Consider the area, facilities, and protection of the vicinity while deciding on your accommodations. Additionally, leverage online structures, together with Airbnb or nearby real assets websites, to locate the high-quality offers and negotiate condominium agreements.

Food prices also can range substantially depending at the holiday spot. Research nearby markets and supermarkets to discover much less costly groceries and put together dinner your meals at domestic. Eating out may be a splendid manner to enjoy the community manner of existence, however it could additionally drain your fee range fast.

Balance your desire for culinary exploration with rate-effective picks.

Finally, medical insurance is a vital attention for virtual nomads. Ensure you have got were given whole health insurance that consists of clinical charges, emergency evacuation, and repatriation. Research the close by healthcare system and determine if you want more coverage or if your present day plan offers suitable sufficient insurance.

"Life is each a formidable journey or not whatever in any respect"

By carefully budgeting and thinking about the rate of residing, you could restriction financial pressure and make the most of your digital nomad manner of existence. Remember to regularly assessment and alter your fee range as your events trade. With proper making plans and monetary manage, you may experience the freedom and versatility of going for walks and residing anywhere inside the international.

"Travel makes one modest, you be aware

what a tiny vicinity you occupy in the

worldwide."

Dealing with Insurance and

Healthcare

One of the vital factors that every digital nomad, expat, or everyone planning to stay and paintings distant places ought to recall is coverage and healthcare.

Ensuring you've got proper insurance and get proper of get admission to to to first-class clinical services is essential in terms of safeguarding your nicely-being and peace of thoughts at the equal time as dwelling foreign places.

When it involves insurance, there are some key areas to popularity on. First and principal, you need to preserve in mind health insurance. Each u.S.A. Of the us has its private healthcare gadget, and it's essential to recognize the way it really works and whether or no longer you are eligible to join up. Some worldwide places may also additionally moreover require you to have local medical medical health insurance as a criminal requirement, whilst others also can assist you to rely upon non-public coverage or international medical medical health insurance plans.

Researching and comparing alternatives to find a coverage that suits your dreams and rate range is critical.

Another crucial insurance attention is tour insurance. As a digital nomad, you could locate your self regularly moving from one u . S . To a few special.

Having entire excursion coverage that covers scientific emergencies, journey cancellations, misplaced baggage, and certainly one of a type unexpected sports is critical. Look for tips that provide worldwide insurance and take into account any specific necessities or barriers that would practice on your manner of life.

Additionally, it is really worth exploring options for personal felony responsibility insurance. This form of coverage protects you in case you by means of risk reason harm or injury to others. It's in particular applicable for virtual nomads who frequently paintings remotely in public areas or have interaction with clients and locals whilst abroad.

Understanding the healthcare system in your selected excursion spot is similarly critical. Research the deliver and extraordinary of scientific services, further to the value of healthcare in that u.S.. Some countries may additionally additionally moreover have brilliant public healthcare structures, at the same time as others can also rely more on non-public healthcare agencies.

Familiarize yourself with the nearby hospitals, clinics, and pharmacies, and hold a list of emergency touch numbers correctly accessible. It's additionally sensible to find out approximately any important vaccinations or fitness precautions you need to take in advance than traveling to a specific u.S..

Lastly, do not forget the significance of preserving a healthful manner of lifestyles at the equal time as dwelling remote places. Prioritize normal exercising, a balanced diet, and good enough sleep to make sure your everyday properly-being. Seek out fitness centers, wholesome food options, and leisure activities to your new vicinity to help your bodily and mental health.

Chapter 4: Finding Accommodation And Transportation

Exploring Different Accommodation Options

When embarking for your journey as a digital nomad, one of the maximum essential factors to recollect is locating suitable lodges. As a international tourist, you've got a plethora of alternatives to choose from, every with its private particular benefits and considerations. In this subchapter, we can explore diverse lodging options, catering specially to the desires of digital nomads, expats, and those seeking to stay and art work foreign places.

1. Short-term Rentals: These are ideal for individuals who pick flexibility and freedom. Platforms like Airbnb, Booking.Com, and VRBO provide a huge type of provided houses, condos, and homes for short-term stays. You can without difficulty discover cushty and low-cost alternatives, regularly with services which include Wi-Fi and laundry centers.

2. Co-residing Spaces: Designed with virtual nomads in mind, co-living regions offer a network-oriented surroundings in which like-minded people can stay, paintings, and collaborate together. These regions often offer shared offerings like coworking regions, communal kitchens, and organized social activities, fostering a sense of camaraderie and networking possibilities.

three. Serviced Apartments: Ideal for the ones in search of a trouble-loose life-style, serviced apartments provide the comforts of home coupled with hotel-like offerings.

These lodges are certainly furnished and organized, presenting house responsibilities, renovation, and concierge offerings. They are in particular famous in most important towns and company hubs.

four. House-Sitting and Home Exchanges: For the adventurous souls, residence-sitting and home exchanges provide unique possibilities to live like a local. Websites like TrustedHousesitters and HomeExchange connect house proprietors with people willing to attend to their houses even as they may be away. This not best presents fee-effective resorts however additionally lets in you to immerse your self within the nearby way of lifestyles.

five. Digital Nomad Retreats: If you crave a based environment that combines paintings and play, virtual nomad retreats might be the proper healthful for you. These organized programs provide accommodations, coworking regions, workshops, and networking sports tailored mainly for digital nomads. They provide an superb way to hook up with like-minded humans even as exploring new places.

6. Long-time period Rentals: Finally, if you are planning to stay in a particular region for an extended period, prolonged-term leases may be a clever desire. Websites like Craigslist, nearby real assets sellers, and Facebook organizations devoted to expats frequently

have listings for homes and homes available for long-term rent.

Negotiating a rent right away with a landlord can from time to time result in extra favorable phrases.

Remember, deciding on the proper lodging is essential for growing a comfortable and efficient surroundings as a digital nomad. Consider your rate range, favored period of stay, location, and private choices to select out the choice that exceptional fits your dreams. Happy exploring!

"Traveling it leaves you

speechless, then turns you right right into a

storyteller."

Tips for Finding Affordable and

Safe Housing

As a digital nomad, finding less luxurious and secure housing is important in your success and ordinary properly-being at the same time as living and working abroad. Whether you're an expat, a person searching for to art work overseas, or truely trying to find to enjoy existence overseas, those tips will assist you navigate the housing market and find out the precise location to name home.

1. Research the Local Rental Market: Before arriving on your chosen holiday spot, conduct thorough studies at the community rental market. Familiarize your self with condominium charges, commonplace utilities fees, and famous neighborhoods. This will offer you with a higher know-how of what to anticipate and help you decide a sensible fee variety.

2. Utilize Online Platforms and Groups: The net is a precious resource for locating less costly and consistent housing. Utilize on line systems which encompass Airbnb, Booking.Com, and nearby real belongings internet web web sites to search for quick time period or prolonged-time period rentals. Additionally, be a part of virtual nomad

groups and boards on social media systems to connect with other like-minded those who can offer treasured insights and guidelines.

three. Consider Co-Living Spaces: Co-living regions have become more and more well-known among virtual nomads.

These areas offer much less high-priced housing options, frequently provided and prepared with essential centers. Additionally, co-dwelling areas provide a enjoy of community, allowing you to connect to specific virtual nomads and extend your network.

4. Reach Out to Local Expats: Expats who've already installation themselves in your preferred excursion spot may be a wealth of understanding. Reach out to nearby expat groups or hook up with expats via social media systems. They can provide valuable recommendation on secure neighborhoods, reliable landlords, and affordable housing alternatives.

5. Prioritize Safety: Safety have to be a pinnacle precedence when searching out housing. Research the crime prices and protection popularity of the neighborhoods you're considering. Additionally, don't forget elements which includes strong building get entry to, properly-lit streets, and proximity to emergency services.

6. Leverage Local Contacts: Building a network of community contacts can drastically assist you in finding lots much less costly and steady housing. Reach out to community specialists, colleagues, or friends who can offer hints or be a part of you with dependable landlords or real property sellers.

7. Negotiate Rental Terms: Don't be afraid to barter rental phrases, specifically for long-time period rentals.

Landlords may be inclined to provide discounted prices or flexible rent agreements, in particular in the course of off-pinnacle seasons. Be prepared to negotiate and advocate for your self to constant the splendid viable deal.

By following those tips, you can discover reasonably-priced and steady housing alternatives that suit your desires as a virtual nomad. Remember to behavior thorough research, make use of online structures and network contacts, prioritize protection, and negotiate apartment terms. With a chunk effort and patience, you may find the ideal home in your preferred holiday spot as you embody the digital nomad way of existence.

"If you agree with you studied adventure is volatile, strive ordinary, it's deadly"

Navigating Transportation in

Foreign Countries

As a digital nomad, one of the maximum thrilling elements of living and working foreign places is exploring its specific manner of existence and immersing yourself in its colorful environment. However, getting round overseas can on occasion be a frightening challenge, particularly in case you're unexpected with the nearby transportation system.

In this subchapter, we're able to manual you via the tremendous statistics of navigating transportation in overseas countries, making sure that you could journey correctly and correctly all through a while overseas.

"Great topics in no way came from

comfort zones."

When it involves deciding on the awesome transportation mode, keep in mind elements at the side of fee, comfort, and protection. For shorter distances, on foot or cycling is probably the most suitable options, permitting you to discover the network neighborhoods and soak within the environment.

However, for longer distances, public transportation is frequently the most fee-green and efficient desire.

Understanding the way to use the community transportation apps, shopping clever playing playing cards, or records the particular rate strategies will make your each day journey a good deal smoother.

While public transportation is usually reliable, it is essential to be aware of any capability scams or protection troubles. Research common scams and pickpocketing techniques for your holiday spot u . S . A ., and take important precautions to shield yourself and your assets. Additionally, preserve in mind that rush hours and peak instances might also motive crowded transportation, so plan your journeys subsequently.

If public transportation does no longer in shape your goals or if you make a decision on greater flexibility, bear in thoughts the use of experience-sharing services or renting a car. However, be privy to using guidelines, avenue situations, and parking availability on your host u.S. Of the usa. International the use of permits can be required in some places, so make certain to accumulate the vital documentation earlier than hitting the street.

Lastly, bear in thoughts to discover opportunity transportation options like shared bicycles or electric powered scooters, which can be turning into an increasing number of popular in many cities international. These green options offer a accessible and a laugh way to navigate thru busy streets and reduce your carbon footprint.

"If you're constantly looking for to be

regular, you can never comprehend how

remarkable you may be."

By reading the art work of navigating transportation in foreign places countries, you may be able to seamlessly discover your new environment, immerse yourself inside the close by lifestyle, and make the maximum of your virtual nomad manner of lifestyles. Remember to live informed, plan in advance, and consist of the adventure that awaits you in each corner of the arena.

"An journey an afternoon continues the physician away."

Understanding Local Transportation Options and Apps

As a virtual nomad embracing the freedom of going for walks and residing everywhere in the global, it is vital to familiarize yourself with the nearby transportation options to be had to you in your preferred vacation spot.

Navigating the neighborhood transportation system efficaciously can considerably enhance your popular enjoy and help you seamlessly integrate into your new environment.

Fortunately, in this digital age, there are numerous transportation apps which could help you in locating and using community transportation offerings effectively.

"Stop demanding approximately the potholes in

the street and experience the adventure"

When arriving in a today's u . S . A . As an expat or virtual nomad, one of the first things you need to do is studies the various transportation alternatives available.

Whether it's public buses, trains, trams, or taxis, expertise the community transportation tool will save you time, cash, and useless stress. Many cities have whole public transportation networks that provide on hand and inexpensive options for getting round town. Familiarize yourself with the routes, schedules, and charge methods for these modes of transportation.

Chapter 5: Embracing The Local Culture And Language

Learning Basic Phrases and

Language Skills

For digital nomads, the capability to speak correctly in awesome international places is essential. Learning essential phrases and language skills not simplest allows you navigate each day existence but additionally enhances your normal experience as you immerse yourself in new cultures. In this subchapter, we are able to explore the importance of language abilities for digital nomads, offer sensible pointers for analyzing a present day day language, and recommend assets that will help you along the manner.

Understanding the Basics: When jogging and living out of the country, it is vital to understand primary phrases and language competencies. These abilities permit you to talk with locals, navigate public transportation, order meals, and address regular conditions genuinely. Learning even a few key phrases can skip a long manner in building connections and making your enjoy greater exciting.

Practical Tips for Learning a New Language: 1. Start with the necessities: Begin thru studying normally used terms, which encompass greetings, polite expressions, and numbers. These will form the muse on your language mastering adventure.

2. Practice with locals: Engaging with locals is an brilliant manner to decorate your language competencies. Don't be afraid to strike up conversations, ask for assist, or be part of language exchange groups. Immersion is often the nice way to investigate a cutting-edge language.

three. Utilize language gaining knowledge of apps: There are numerous language learning apps to be had that provide interactive classes, flashcards, and pronunciation wearing activities.

Duolingo, Babbel, and Rosetta Stone are famous alternatives among virtual nomads.

four. Take language commands: Consider enrolling in community language education or hiring a private train. Structured commands can offer a extra comprehensive information of grammar, vocabulary, and pronunciation.

five. Immerse your self in nearby media: Watch films, be aware of podcasts, and study books or newspapers inside the local language. Surrounding yourself with the language will help you boom an ear for it and enhance your statistics.

"There is not anything extra secure than flying,

it's the crashing that's risky."

Recommended Resources:

1. Phrasebooks and language dictionaries: Carry a pocket-sized phrasebook or use language translation apps to have brief get right of entry to to vital terms and vocabulary.

2. Language mastering web sites: Websites like FluentU, Memrise, and Lingoda provide interactive education, sports activities sports, and language alternate possibilities.

three. Language Meetup companies: Meetup.Com and distinct comparable structures host language change activities in which you could exercising speakme with locals or extraordinary language freshmen.

"Jet Lag is for Amateurs."

Remember, reading a brand new language takes time and consistent attempt. Don't be discouraged through way of initial troubles. Embrace the venture, exercising frequently, and feature a laugh every small milestone. By making an funding in language abilities, you will be better organized to navigate super international places, forge full-size connections, and truly include the digital nomad way of life.

"I need I had in no way long long long past journeying."

Said no person ever.

Understanding Cultural Etiquette and Customs

In present day interconnected world, being a digital nomad gives great possibilities to paintings and live everywhere within the international. However, it is essential to recognize that every u.S. Has its specific cultural etiquette and customs. Adapting to those customs is critical for building sturdy relationships, respecting network traditions, and thriving in a latest environment. In this subchapter, we are capable of discover the importance of knowledge cultural etiquette and customs as a virtual nomad.

"The vital trouble is to in no way save you questioning. Curiosity has its private

purpose for present"

Firstly, cultural etiquette refers to the unwritten rules and norms that govern social interactions indoors a selected way of life.

These norms can also include greetings, gestures, appropriate behavior, and communication styles. By information and respecting those customs, virtual nomads can foster excellent relationships with locals and avoid inadvertently offending others.

One of the number one steps to statistics cultural etiquette is to do thorough research in advance than arriving in a new america of the usa. Learn approximately their traditions, social norms, and values. This knowledge will assist you navigate numerous situations, which include greetings, present-giving, and consuming etiquette. For example, in some cultures, it can be widespread to do away with your footwear in advance than entering a domestic, at the equal time as in others, it could be taken into consideration disrespectful to reveal the soles of your toes.

Additionally, conversation patterns can vary appreciably among cultures. Some cultures can also price direct and assertive conversation, even as others prioritize subtlety and indirectness. By recognizing those versions, digital nomads can adapt their verbal exchange fashion to efficiently speak with locals and avoid misunderstandings.

Furthermore, expertise cultural etiquette isn't always confined to social interactions however additionally extends to the place of work. Different global places have their very very own professional customs, which incorporates suitable dress codes, punctuality expectancies, and negotiation patterns. Being privy to the ones customs will assist virtual nomads navigate expert environments and construct a hit going for walks relationships.

Lastly, it is vital to method cultural variations with an open mind and a willingness to study. Embrace the possibility to immerse yourself in a contemporary way of lifestyles, engage with locals, and ask questions. By displaying recognize and hobby, you may no longer first-class advantage a deeper information of the community customs however additionally assemble big connections with human beings from great backgrounds.

In stop, statistics cultural etiquette and customs is essential for digital nomads trying to artwork and stay overseas. By familiarizing themselves with community customs, virtual nomads can navigate social interactions, assemble robust relationships, and thrive in a new cultural environment. Embracing cultural versions with an open thoughts will no longer first-class boom their studies however moreover make contributions to a a fulfillment and appealing existence as a virtual nomad.

Making Local Connections and

Building a Support Network

As a digital nomad, one of the maximum valuable sources you can have is a robust assist network on your new region. Building close by connections now not exceptional allows you navigate the annoying situations of residing and jogging distant places but moreover enriches your experience with the aid of the usage of immersing you inside the nearby way of life and network. In this subchapter, we can discover strategies for making close by connections and constructing a assist community as a digital nomad.

"I must as an alternative very personal a hint and observe

the arena than very very very own the area and

see a touch of it."

One of the primary steps to building a guide network is to are seeking out out expat corporations on your new location.

These organizations are often complete of like-minded people who have faced similar challenges and may provide treasured recommendation and aid. Attend network expat activities, be part of online forums, and hook up with expat businesses on social media structures to begin networking with fellow virtual nomads and expats.

In addition to expat communities, it is critical to take some time to connect to locals. Engaging with locals no longer most effective lets in you combine into the area people however additionally offers an opportunity to discover about the manner of lifestyles, language, and customs of your new domestic. Participate in nearby sports activities, volunteer for network projects, or take language instructions to satisfy and have interaction with locals.

Networking occasions and coworking regions additionally can be notable places to make close by connections. These areas are frequently packed with professionals from numerous backgrounds, along side locals who are interested by meeting new people and expanding their network.

Attend employer-associated activities, workshops, and meetings to hook up with professionals to your subject and functionality customers or collaborators.

Another effective method is to find out a mentor or be a part of a mastermind corporation. A mentor can provide guidance, manual, and precious insights primarily based absolutely totally on their own reviews as a virtual nomad or expat. A mastermind group, however, allows you to connect with a collection of folks who percentage similar goals and can provide extraordinary views and solutions to the annoying situations you can face.

Finally, leverage on line structures and social media to connect to considered one of a kind virtual nomads and expats worldwide. Join on line corporations, participate in webinars, and engage in discussions on systems like Facebook agencies, Reddit, or specialised forums. These virtual connections can offer a sense of belonging and help, even supposing bodily remote out of your network.

Building neighborhood connections and a assist community as a virtual nomad takes time and effort, however the blessings are worthwhile. By connecting with fellow expats, locals, professionals, mentors, and digital companies, you can not high-quality discover assist in navigating the annoying conditions of living and going for walks overseas but moreover create lifelong friendships and recollections a awesome manner to enhance your virtual nomad journey.

Exploring Local Cuisine and

Experiences

One of the most interesting factors of dwelling and running as a virtual nomad out of the country is the opportunity to indulge in the close by cuisine and immerse yourself in particular cultural reviews. From savoring fragrant avenue food to attending traditional fairs, exploring the close by food scene may be a lovable adventure for expats, people who need to art work foreign places, and digital nomads.

Food has a way of connecting human beings, and trying new dishes can provide a deeper facts of a rustic's manner of life and traditions.

"It is higher to see a few element as soon as than to pay attention about it 1000 times."

Whether you discover your self in the bustling streets of Bangkok, the colourful markets of Mexico City, or the old style cafes of Paris, each excursion spot gives its non-public gastronomic treasures. Embrace the possibility to step out of your consolation area and find out culinary gem stones which may be off the crushed direction.

One of the exceptional methods to find out the neighborhood cuisine is via using way of indulging in road meals. These humble and actual dishes regularly tell a tale of the location's history and facts. Venture into the bustling night time markets, in which the tantalizing smells of scorching skewers, steaming bowls of noodles, and freshly baked pastries will trap your taste buds. Engage with locals, ask for his or her recommendations, and be open to trying dishes you can in no manner have encountered in advance than.

In addition to avenue meals, ensure to immerse your self in the nearby meals way of life with the aid of the use of manner of ingesting at conventional eating locations. Seek out family-run institutions which have been serving their signature dishes for generations. By helping the ones community institutions, you not incredible have the possibility to pride in extraordinary flavors but furthermore make contributions to the renovation of culinary traditions.

Beyond meals, exploring close by tales can enhance your virtual nomad adventure. Attend conventional gala's, in which you may witness colorful parades, colorful costumes, and captivating performances.

These celebrations provide a glimpse into the coronary heart and soul of a life-style, permitting you to connect to the local people on a deeper diploma.

To make the most of your exploration, go through in thoughts taking cooking schooling to discover ways to recreate a number of your chosen neighborhood dishes. Not only will this provide you with a modern day potential, however it will furthermore assist you to bring a bit of your selected excursion spot decrease again domestic with you.

In quit, as a virtual nomad, embracing and exploring the nearby cuisine and critiques is an important part of completely immersing yourself in a today's usa of the usa. Whether it's miles indulging in road food, ingesting at conventional ingesting places, or attending cultural festivals, these research will deepen your knowledge of the nearby culture and create lasting memories. So, step out of your comfort quarter, try new flavors, and dive into the wealthy tapestry of food and evaluations that each vacation spot has to offer.

Chapter 6: Staying Healthy And Balanced As A Digital Nomad

Prioritizing Physical and Mental

Well-being

In the short-paced digital global we live in today, it is easy to get stuck up in the hustle and bustle of difficult paintings, in particular for virtual nomads. However, it is critical to maintain in thoughts that your bodily and mental nicely-being must constantly be a pinnacle priority. In this subchapter, we are capable of find out the significance of looking after your self and provide practical suggestions on the way to preserve a healthy way of life on the identical time as dwelling the virtual nomad way of existence.

"When became the very last time you in all likelihood did

some aspect for the primary time."

Physical well-being is the inspiration for a fulfilling and a achievement life as a virtual nomad. It is vital to installation healthful behavior on the manner to beneficial resource your common fitness.

Regular exercise is crucial to preserving physical health and preventing the sedentary nature of far flung paintings.

Explore wonderful types of exercising that you experience and can effects include into your nomadic way of existence, which includes yoga, strolling, or trekking. Make it a detail to stretch and skip your body often at some degree inside the day to prevent muscle stiffness and fatigue.

In addition to workout, paying attention to your nutrients is essential. As a virtual nomad, it could be tempting to depend upon short and available meals, but be aware of the impact those alternatives ought to your regular health. Prioritize entire additives, stop end result, greens, and lean proteins for your healthy eating plan. Plan your meals and snacks earlier to keep away from relying on dangerous options at the same time as you're at the pass.

While bodily well-being is crucial, intellectual properly-being is similarly crucial for digital nomads. The nature of some distance off paintings can be preserving aside and traumatic at instances.

Prioritize self-care sports activities that sell mental nicely-being, which consist of meditation, journaling, or accomplishing interests you experience. Cultivate a assist network of like-minded folks who recognize the disturbing situations of the digital nomad manner of lifestyles.

Balance is high in terms of retaining bodily and intellectual well-being as a digital nomad. Set obstacles amongst work and personal life to avoid burnout. Create a delegated workspace this is separate out of your residing location to hold a healthful work-lifestyles balance. Disconnect from technology regularly to recharge and rejuvenate. Engage in sports activities that deliver you satisfaction and could will permit you to discover the modern-day environments you discover your self in.

Remember, your health and nicely-being must normally be a difficulty. By prioritizing bodily and intellectual properly-being, you'll be better equipped to thrive as a digital nomad and truly experience the liberty and flexibility that carries residing and running everywhere inside the international.

"Someday I'm going to be unfastened and

I'm going to adventure the location."

Finding Fitness and Wellness

Facilities Abroad

Living and working as a digital nomad overseas can be an extraordinary adventure, but it's miles critical to prioritize your fitness and nicely-being at the same time as on the road. Staying fit and preserving a healthy way of existence is important for desired well-being and productivity. Fortunately, there are numerous health and nicely-being centers available global that cater to the desires of virtual nomads.

"We adventure not to interrupt out life but for existence no longer to get away us."

When looking for fitness and wellness centers foreign places, it is vital to recall your unique desires and options. Different global locations have diverse stages of health subculture and access to health facilities, so it's vital to do your studies earlier than arriving. Here are some guidelines that will help you discover the appropriate health and well being facilities at the identical time as dwelling and running overseas: 1. Research nearby gyms and fitness centers: Before arriving in a cutting-edge-day u . S . A ., studies and make a listing of network gyms and fitness centers. The internet is a treasured useful aid for finding facts, opinions, and tips. Look for centers that provide flexible club alternatives or day passes to deal with your nomadic way of life.

2. Consider outdoor sports activities: Some global locations offer a plethora of out of doors sports that may double as health physical video games. Consider carrying out sports activities in conjunction with hiking, surfing, yoga on the beach, or cycling to find out new locations on the equal time as getting your workout.

3. Utilize coworking areas with fitness facilities: Many coworking areas worldwide now offer fitness centers inner their premises. These regions cater specially to virtual nomads and frequently offer flexible memberships that include get right of access to to each workspace and health centers.

four. Explore close by nicely being practices: Embrace the community way of life and find out conventional health practices to be had on your host united states of america. This have to consist of yoga, meditation, martial arts, or maybe community spa treatments.

Engaging inside the ones practices no longer handiest contributes to your bodily fitness but moreover gives a very particular cultural enjoy.

five. Connect with like-minded individuals: Join digital nomad companies online or attend networking events in your new location. These communities can provide precious insights and pointers for health and fitness facilities that cater especially to the dreams of digital nomads.

Remember, keeping a healthy manner of lifestyles is a non-public responsibility. By prioritizing your fitness and health, you may enhance your productiveness, reduce stress, and revel in a satisfying digital nomad way of life. So, whether or no longer or not you pick out hitting the fitness center, going for walks in the direction of yoga, or exploring out of doors sports, there are loads of alternatives to be had to help you stay suit and properly on the same time as dwelling and strolling foreign places.

"Don't pay attention to what they may be saying,

go see"

Coping with Loneliness and Homesickness

Living a nomadic lifestyle as a virtual nomad may be pretty worthwhile, but it's miles now not with out its stressful conditions. One of the maximum common struggles confronted by expats, people who art work abroad, and those who choose to live and artwork foreign places is handling loneliness and homesickness. In this subchapter, we can explore realistic strategies and suggestions that will help you navigate the ones emotions and hold a extremely good mindset at the identical time as for your digital nomad journey.

"Don't Quit Your Day Dream"

First and important, it's important to widely recognized that feeling lonely or homesick is absolutely ordinary.

Adjusting to a brand new surroundings, culture, and social circle takes time, and it's adequate to miss the familiarity and comfort of home. Remember that you're no longer on my own in those feelings, as many virtual nomads have professional comparable emotions.

To fight loneliness, make an effort to construct a sturdy aid network. Seek out network expat agencies, coworking spaces, or on-line boards in which you can connect to like-minded humans. Engage in sports that interest you, along with turning into a member of a sports activities club or attending meetups, to fulfill new humans and increase your social circle. Additionally, hold normal touch with buddies and own family lower decrease returned home thru video calls or social media structures to live related.

Homesickness may be alleviated via using developing a feel of home everywhere you pass. Surround your self with familiar devices or mementos that deliver you comfort, together with photos or a favorite blanket. Establish sporting events that provide you with a enjoy of stability and normalcy, whether or no longer or no longer it's cooking a familiar meal or schooling a each day exercising ordinary. Engage in self-care sports activities that promote rest, together with meditation, journaling, or exploring nearby nature spots.

Finding a stability among solitude and socializing is crucial. While it's far vital to encompass new stories and make connections, don't underestimate the power of on my own time. Use this opportunity for self-reflected photograph, non-public boom, and pursuing pursuits or pastimes that deliver you satisfaction.

Embrace the liberty that consists of being a virtual nomad and use it to create a satisfying life for yourself.

Remember, coping with loneliness and homesickness is a gadget that calls for staying power and self-compassion.

Be kind to your self and permit yourself to sense the emotions that rise up. By implementing the ones techniques and maintaining a outstanding thoughts-set, you can navigate the worrying conditions of loneliness and homesickness even as embracing the exceptional possibilities that include being a virtual nomad.

"Try to Be a Rainbow in Someone

Else's Cloud"

Balancing Work and Personal Life

In modern-day speedy-paced international, attaining a wholesome paintings-lifestyles stability has come to be increasingly difficult. This is in particular real for digital nomads people who have embraced a region-impartial way of life, permitting them to work and stay anywhere within the global.

As an expat, a person proceeding to paintings distant places, or actually someone yearning to stay and paintings remote places, locating equilibrium amongst your professional and private existence is vital to hold your happiness and productivity. In this subchapter, we are able to discover powerful techniques and practical pointers to help you correctly balance your art work and private lifestyles as a virtual nomad.

"Where to subsequent?"

First and crucial, it's miles important to installation smooth limitations among artwork and private time. While the attraction of consistent adventure and exploration may be tempting, dedicating specific hours each day absolutely to work can growth your productiveness and prevent burnout. Setting a schedule and sticking to it will can help you interest on your expert duties whilst furthermore ensuring you have got ok time for rest, rest, and personal pursuits.

Moreover, as a digital nomad, it is vital to create a chosen workspace anywhere you are. This can be as clean as finding a quiet corner in a café or making an investment in a transportable desk setup. A devoted workspace allows create a mental separation among your paintings and private lifestyles, permitting you to replace into work mode at the same time as desired and switch off whilst it is time to unwind.

Additionally, incorporating self-care practices into your each day routine is critical for preserving a wholesome artwork-life balance. Prioritize sports which includes workout, meditation, and spending time outside to rejuvenate your mind and frame. These practices will now not best enhance your ordinary properly-being however furthermore improve your productiveness and creativity.

Furthermore, nurturing social connections is essential for the virtual nomad manner of lifestyles. Actively are seeking out out neighborhood groups, be a part of coworking areas, and take part in networking activities to satisfy like-minded people.

Building a sturdy help community will now not handiest provide you with a revel in of belonging but additionally offer possibilities for collaboration and personal boom.

"To Travel is to Live"

Lastly, it's far vital to periodically re-study and adjust your priorities. As your instances and dreams evolve, so must your technique to artwork and private lifestyles. Continually evaluating what simply subjects to you could help you're making informed selections and keep a harmonious stability.

Chapter 7: Overcoming Common Digital Nomad Challenges

Dealing with Internet and Technology Issues

In contemporary international, wherein generation has emerge as an critical a part of our lives, it's far crucial for virtual nomads to be nicely-ready to handle internet and technology troubles. Whether you're an expat, a person who desires to art work distant places, or in reality someone who dreams of dwelling and operating foreign places, data the manner to navigate these demanding situations is important.

One of the maximum huge issues for digital nomads is net get right of get admission to to. Without a dependable internet connection, it may be hard to work effectively and stay related with clients and buddies.

Therefore, it's miles vital to research and pick out out lodges with stable and excessive-pace net get right of access to. Look for places that mainly cater to virtual nomads, as they often provide co-going for walks areas and reliable Wi-Fi.

However, no matter a dependable net connection, technical troubles can despite the fact that rise up. It is wise to have a backup plan in place, collectively with a cellular hotspot or a nearby café with unfastened Wi-Fi. This guarantees that you can rapid transfer to an exchange internet deliver if wanted.

Another not unusual undertaking confronted with the beneficial resource of virtual nomads is staying up to date with era. New gadgets and software are continuously rising, and it could be overwhelming to preserve song of all the upgrades.

Stay associated with on line organizations and forums that cater to virtual nomads to live knowledgeable about the present day technology tendencies and equipment that could enhance your productiveness and ordinary overall performance.

"To adventure is to find out that

every body is wrong approximately extraordinary

nations."

Cybersecurity is some other trouble that must no longer be disregarded. As a virtual nomad, you want to take more precautions to protect your sensitive statistics and private statistics. Utilize sturdy and unique passwords, allow - element authentication, and don't forget using a virtual personal community (VPN) to solid your net connection at the same time as having access to public Wi-Fi hotspots.

"The international is modified by using the usage of your

example, not your opinion."

Lastly, it is essential to have a mind-set of adaptability at the same time as managing net and generation problems.

Embrace the reality that things might not commonly move as deliberate, and be organized to troubleshoot and find opportunity solutions. Patience and resourcefulness are crucial traits for virtual nomads while faced with technical annoying conditions.

In give up, as a digital nomad, being prepared to cope with net and technology troubles is vital for a a hit and fun way of lifestyles. From ensuring strong internet get right of entry to to staying up to date with the extremely-modern-day era upgrades and protecting your cybersecurity, taking proactive steps will will permit you to paintings and live everywhere in the global with no problem and self assurance. Remember, with the right attitude and training, you can overcome any challenge that comes your way.

Managing Work-Life Balance in

Different Time Zones

One of the most exciting components of being a digital nomad is the potential to paintings and stay anywhere within the world.

However, this freedom regularly comes with the project of handling art work-lifestyles balance, particularly even as you find out your self in terrific time zones. In this subchapter, we're able to discover some realistic strategies that will help you preserve a healthful paintings-existence stability whilst navigating distinct time zones as a digital nomad.

"You need to be the trade you preference to

see inside the international."

The first step in handling paintings-life stability throughout time zones is to installation a ordinary that works for you. Consider your paintings hours and the time quarter of your clients or colleagues. Create a agenda that lets in for uninterrupted artwork all through overlapping hours and dedicated non-public time while the time zones vary. This will assist you keep a feel of shape and make certain you have got had been given time for every art work and private sports.

Communication is pinnacle even as strolling in some unspecified time in the future of splendid time zones. Clearly speak your availability and desired strategies of verbal exchange for your customers or colleagues.

Establish a machine for sharing updates, deadlines, and crucial information, making sure that everyone is on the equal internet net web page however the time versions.

Utilize system like undertaking manipulate software program application, video conferencing, and instant messaging apps to facilitate efficient conversation.

Take benefit of your flexibility as a virtual nomad to time desk breaks and downtime throughout your day.

Explore the neighborhood way of lifestyles, take pleasure for your hobbies, or absolutely loosen up and recharge. Remember that work-existence stability isn't always pretty a good deal art work; it's far about making time for yourself and experiencing the thrill of residing in a specific the us of the us.

To overcome the traumatic conditions of going for walks in notable time zones, remember adopting a bendy paintings affiliation. Negotiate together with your clients or employers to set up possibility art work hours that align better with the time location you are currently in. This can assist lower the impact of time variations in your paintings and personal existence.

Lastly, prioritize self-care and properly-being. It's smooth to get stuck up in paintings whilst you're continuously on the glide, but it's miles essential to attend to your physical and intellectual health. Make time for exercise, devour nutritious food, and get enough sleep. Establishing a ordinary self-care everyday will assist you live energized and focused but the demanding conditions of numerous time zones.

In give up, managing artwork-lifestyles stability in splendid time zones is a ability that each virtual nomad should draw close. By putting in region a everyday, preserving powerful verbal exchange, embracing flexibility, and prioritizing self-care, you may efficiently navigate the stressful situations that include operating in the course of diverse time zones.

Remember, the key is finding a stability that lets in you to revel in the blessings of being a digital nomad at the same time as thriving professionally and in my opinion.

Handling Visa Extensions and

Immigration Matters

For digital nomads and people searching out to paintings and stay distant places, navigating the complexities of visa extensions and immigration subjects may be a daunting mission. However, with the proper records and steerage, this system may be streamlined and plausible. This subchapter objectives to provide practical advice and critical information to assist expats, aspiring global human beings, and digital nomads in effectively handling visa extensions and immigration subjects.

"There's a dawn and sundown every

unmarried day, and that they're honestly

free. Don't pass over so plenty of them."

Understanding the Basics:

Before delving into the specifics, it's miles critical to apprehend the critical thoughts surrounding visa extensions and immigration topics. This includes familiarizing oneself with the only of a type varieties of visas, visa requirements, and the easy techniques concerned in extending a visa. Additionally, knowledge the community immigration criminal tips and recommendations of the holiday spot u . S . Is crucial for a clean transition.

Planning Ahead:

Proper planning and training are key to fending off useless pressure and complications. It is recommended to begin amassing all the required files properly in advance and live knowledgeable about any adjustments in immigration legal recommendations or pointers. Researching and consulting with immigration criminal professionals or expert businesses can provide precious insights and assist for the duration of the machine.

Navigating the Visa Extension Process: Each united states of america has its very very own particular techniques and requirements for visa extensions. This subchapter will offer step-via-step guidance on the manner to navigate those strategies efficaciously. From filling out application paperwork to gathering supporting documents, we will offer sensible recommendations and advice to make sure a a success visa extension.

Overcoming Immigration Challenges: Immigration topics can every now and then gift surprising demanding situations. This subchapter will address common problems that virtual nomads and expats might also moreover moreover come upon, alongside facet language limitations, cultural variations, or bureaucratic hurdles. Practical strategies and assets can be furnished to assist triumph over the ones boundaries and restriction capability setbacks.

Seeking Professional Assistance:

While it's miles feasible to address visa extensions and immigration topics independently, trying to find expert help can frequently simplify the gadget and provide peace of mind. In this subchapter, we're able to spotlight the benefits of hiring immigration legal professionals or professional organizations to manual people through the complexities of immigration laws and approaches.

Conclusion:

Handling visa extensions and immigration subjects is an essential thing of the virtual nomad life-style and working foreign places.

By expertise the basics, making plans in advance, navigating the visa extension approach, overcoming worrying conditions, and in search of expert help on the same time as wanted, human beings can efficaciously embark on their international art work adventure.

This subchapter objectives to equip expats, aspiring worldwide employees, and virtual nomads with the vital information and equipment to navigate the intricacies of visa extensions and immigration subjects, making sure a persevering with and profitable enjoy.

"Life isn't about finding your self. Life is ready growing your self."

Coping with Unforeseen Challenges

and Emergencies

Living a virtual nomad lifestyle can be each exhilarating and profitable, allowing people to paintings and stay everywhere in the worldwide. However, it isn't without its annoying situations. One of the critical aspect factors of being a a fulfillment digital nomad is studying the manner to address unexpected annoying situations and emergencies which can get up for the duration of your journey. In this subchapter, we are able to find out a few valuable strategies to help you navigate thru the ones sudden situations.

"If your deliver doesn't are to be had in, swim out to it."

1. Building a Support Network: As a virtual nomad, it's far vital to installation a resource network, every on-line and offline. Join expat communities, hook up with like-minded individuals, and construct relationships with fellow digital nomads. These networks can offer you with valuable advice, help, and assist for the duration of hard instances.

2. Emergency Fund: Create an emergency fund mainly for unexpected conditions. This fund ought to cover clinical emergencies, unexpected tour fees, and any surprising instances that could upward thrust up. By

having a economic protection net, you can have peace of mind and the capability to cope with emergencies with out disrupting your art work or way of life.

"Without new studies,

a few thing inner us sleeps. The

sleeper should wake up."

three. Travel and Health Insurance: Securing whole adventure and medical insurance is crucial for virtual nomads. Ensure that your coverage insurance includes emergency hospital therapy, evacuation, and repatriation. This will shield you financially and offer get proper of access to to pleasant healthcare, regardless of wherein you're inside the international.

four. Developing Resilience: Being adaptable and resilient is fundamental to dealing with surprising demanding situations. Embrace the mind-set that setbacks are possibilities for increase. Learn out of your opinions, discover answers, and live flexible for your approach.

By growing resilience, you may be higher geared up to cope with any barriers that come your manner.

"Those who comply with the group

usually get lost in it."

5. Planning for Contingencies: While being spontaneous is a part of the enchantment of the digital nomad way of life, it's miles vital to plot for contingencies.

Research your excursion spot, apprehend the community criminal guidelines and customs, and characteristic a backup plan in case of emergencies. This will assist you mitigate risks and navigate thru unforeseen situations effectively.

6. Seeking Professional Help: In some instances, unforeseen worrying situations also can require professional help. Whether it's far felony recommendation, scientific assist, or logistical help, do now not hesitate to reap out to experts who attention on managing expats and virtual nomads. They can offer you

with the steering and expertise wanted to overcome any unexpected limitations.

"This coronary coronary coronary heart of mine modified into made to

journey this international"

By imposing those strategies, you may be nicely-organized to cope with unexpected annoying situations and emergencies as a digital nomad. Remember, on the equal time as unexpected conditions can be stressful, in addition they present possibilities for non-public and professional increase. Embrace the nomadic manner of life with self guarantee, knowing which you have the equipment and mind-set to cope with any situation that comes your way.

"Because whilst you stop and look

Around, this life is pretty exquisite."

Chapter 8: Building A Sustainable Digital Nomad Career

Networking and Building Professional

Relationships

In present day day interconnected international, networking and constructing professional relationships have turn out to be critical capabilities for the current-day digital nomad. Whether you're an expat, a person searching for to art work overseas, or in reality yearning to live and art work out of the country, the power of networking can't be underestimated.

This subchapter will delve into the significance of networking, strategies for constructing strong professional relationships, and the manner to leverage the ones connections to beautify your profession as a digital nomad.

"The Impulse to Travel is one of the

hopeful signs and symptoms of life"

Networking is the vital issue to unlocking opportunities, each non-public and expert, in a present day environment. By connecting with locals, fellow expats, and professionals in various industries, you could tap proper into a big wealth of facts, resources, and capability collaborations. However, effective networking goes beyond in truth gathering business enterprise playing playing cards or LinkedIn connections. It requires true engagement, active participation, and a willingness to offer as tons as you got.

To build robust professional relationships, it's miles essential to undertake an open and approachable mind-set. Attend community meetups, meetings, and industry activities to satisfy like-minded individuals and boom your community. Seek out on line organizations and boards particular to your vicinity of interest as a virtual nomad to hook up with others who percent your passion and can provide valuable insights.

Remember that networking is a two-manner street, so be organized to offer cost to others with the useful resource of using providing your know-how, information, or help each time possible.

Once you've got got installation a community, it is important to nurture the ones relationships. Stay in contact together along with your contacts often via email, social media, or perhaps video calls. Show right interest of their artwork, initiatives, and achievements. Engage in sizeable conversations and offer guide on every occasion you could. By constructing a popularity as a reliable and useful expert, you growth the possibility of receiving referrals, collaborations, and task opportunities.

As a virtual nomad, the potential to leverage your community is critical on your profession success. Your connections can provide close by insights, advocate system opportunities, or maybe provide a place to live in a trendy metropolis or united states. By tapping into those belongings, you may navigate the demanding situations of strolling and dwelling remote places extra correctly.

In stop, networking and constructing expert relationships are critical capabilities for any virtual nomad. By actively engaging with others, imparting price, and nurturing your connections, you may unlock a worldwide of possibilities and decorate your profession as you work and stay everywhere in the worldwide. Embrace the power of networking, and watch as your professional adventure as a virtual nomad takes flight.

"Let's discover a few beautiful region to

wander off"

Developing Multiple Streams of

Income

In current rapid-paced and interconnected international, the idea of a traditional 9-to-5 task is unexpectedly evolving.

More and extra humans are seeking out possibility approaches to earn a dwelling even as embracing a place-independent lifestyle. This subchapter delves into the significance of developing more than one streams of earnings, specifically tailor-made for virtual nomads the ones intrepid folks that choose out to paintings and stay everywhere in the international.

"I'm in love with cities I've in no manner

been to and those I've in no manner met."

As an expat or a person needing to art work abroad, the potential to generate a couple of streams of income turns into paramount. Relying on a unmarried supply of income can be volatile, mainly whilst you are in another country. By diversifying your income streams, you now not awesome increase your monetary stability but additionally benefit the freedom to discover new possibilities and adapt to changing instances.

One of the primary steps to developing multiple income streams is to find out your competencies and passions. As a virtual nomad, you have got were given the advantage of being capable of paintings remotely, which opens up a worldwide of opportunities.

Consider the digital marketplace freelancing structures, a ways flung approach forums, and on line marketplaces

in which you can provide your abilties to a worldwide target market.

Whether you're a proficient author, photograph fashion fashion designer, programmer, or marketer, there are various opportunities to monetize your know-how.

Additionally, leveraging the energy of the net can will permit you to create passive earnings streams. This can also need to include growing and promoting digital products which include e-books, on-line guides, or inventory pix. You also can find out accomplice advertising and advertising, in which you earn a price for promoting services or products that align together with your region of hobby.

Another street to find out is building your own on-line corporation. This may be an e-commerce store, dropshipping task, or perhaps a blog that generates profits thru advertising or subsidized content material cloth material. The opportunities are endless, and with willpower and perseverance, you could flip your ardour proper right into a worthwhile task.

"Travel...the top notch way to be misplaced and

observed on the equal time."

However, it is vital to be conscious that developing a couple of streams of profits requires careful making plans and time management. Balancing special profits streams might also moreover require prioritization and the ability to delegate duties effectively. It's important to reputation at the earnings streams that align collectively with your lengthy-term desires and provide the most capability for boom.

In cease, as a digital nomad or someone thinking about a life distant places, growing more than one streams of income is vital for financial balance and freedom. By diversifying your profits property, you not brilliant restriction dangers however additionally maximize possibilities for boom and exploration. Embrace the virtual age, leverage your abilities and passions, and build a lifestyles that allows you to artwork and stay everywhere inside the global.

Investing in Skill Development and

Continual Learning

As a virtual nomad, one of the maximum valuable belongings you can personal is a diverse capacity set. In latest speedy-paced and ever-evolving global, staying in advance of the curve and constantly enhancing your skills is not handiest crucial but additionally quite worthwhile. Investing in capability development and persistent analyzing opens up a worldwide of opportunities for expats, those who want to art work overseas, and those meaning to stay and paintings overseas.

"The adventure is my domestic."

One of the critical element benefits of being a digital nomad is the capability to artwork remotely, which regularly requires competencies in diverse virtual equipment and generation. By making an funding time and effort into gaining facts of new software software, programming languages, or on line advertising and marketing and advertising strategies, you may beautify your expert profile and stick out from the competition. This not simplest will increase your opportunities of finding a long way off art work however moreover lets in you to command better costs.

Continual studying furthermore plays a essential function in adapting to the ever-changing wishes of the device market. As technology advances and industries remodel, the capabilities that had been as quickly as in name for may additionally additionally turn out to be out of date.

By making an investment in capabilities improvement, you role your self as a lifelong learner who is constantly prepared to evolve and thrive in any surroundings. This flexibility is especially useful for expats and digital nomads, because it permits them to pivot their careers and explore new possibilities as they flow into from one u.S. To some other.

Moreover, continual analyzing has a big effect on personal boom and delight. By developing your understanding and obtaining new skills, you no longer splendid gain a experience of achievement however moreover broaden your horizons. Learning a cutting-edge language, as an example, will allow you to integrate into the nearby subculture, set up deeper connections with the network, and enhance your commonplace experience residing abroad.

To invest in potential development and chronic gaining knowledge of, it is important to emerge as privy to your strengths and regions for development. Research the talents which can be in immoderate call for inner your enterprise and find out numerous getting to know assets such as on line courses, workshops, or mentorship programs. Additionally, networking with like-minded humans and turning into a member of professional corporations can provide precious insights and opportunities for boom.

In end, making an investment in ability development and persistent reading is a critical element of being a a fulfillment digital nomad. By staying adaptable, constantly enhancing your talents set, and embracing lifelong analyzing, you may enhance your professional opportunities, adapt to converting hobby markets, and enjoy non-public increase. So, capture the possibility to put money into yourself and release a worldwide of possibilities as you determine and stay anywhere inside the international.

"It's a massive global on hand, it'd be a disgrace not to experience it."

Planning for the Future and Long-

Term Goals

As a digital nomad, you have got the ideal opportunity to paintings and stay anywhere inside the global. This way of existence gives widespread freedom and flexibility, however it additionally requires cautious planning and hobby for the future. In this subchapter, we're capable of find out the importance of making plans for the future and setting extended-time period wants to make certain a successful and fulfilling lifestyles as a virtual nomad.

"You can shake the sand from your

shoes, however no longer out of your soul."

One of the number one steps in planning for the destiny is to evaluate your economic scenario. As a digital nomad, your income might also additionally variety or come from more than one belongings. It is crucial to create a budget that takes into attention your costs, along with accommodations, transportation, healthcare, and monetary monetary financial savings for retirement.

Consider operating with a monetary advertising and advertising and marketing representative who makes a speciality of strolling with expats or virtual nomads that will help you create a strong financial plan.

In addition to monetary planning, it's miles essential to set prolonged-time period desires to your non-public and professional life.

Ask your self what you desire to achieve inside the next 5, ten, or many years. Do you want to begin your non-public commercial organisation, make bigger new talents, or establish a base in a selected u.S.? Setting clean dreams will assist you live focused and stimulated to make the important steps to benefit them.

As a digital nomad, it's also critical to preserve in mind your prolonged-time period lifestyle alternatives. Do you notice yourself settling down in a specific place or persevering with to adventure indefinitely? Understanding your goals and alternatives will assist you are making knowledgeable picks and create a lifestyle that aligns together with your lengthy-time period goals.

Furthermore, planning for the future furthermore includes considering your personal and professional improvement. Consider making an funding in non-stop reading and obtaining new capabilities as a manner to decorate your far flung art work skills. This want to incorporate taking over line guides, attending meetings, or becoming a member of professional networks in your preferred location.

"Travel isn't always about taking, it is about soaking up the beauty of the world. "

Finally, take into account to plot on your typical well-being.

Living as a digital nomad can now and again be isolating and tough. Make sure to prioritize your mental and physical health through way of searching out social connections, training self-care, and locating a stability amongst paintings and leisure.

In end, planning for the destiny and setting prolonged-term desires is essential for any virtual nomad. By assessing your economic scenario, setting easy desires, thinking about your manner of existence options, and making an investment in private and expert development, you can create a fulfilling and a hit existence as a digital nomad.

Remember, the key is to be proactive and adaptable as you navigate the ever-converting landscape of some distance flung artwork and worldwide living.

Chapter 9: Repatriation And Transitioning

Knowing when its miles Time to Transition

Making the choice to become a virtual nomad and artwork and stay anywhere in the international is genuinely interesting. The freedom and versatility that encompass this manner of existence are incredible. However, like numerous critical life transition, it's critical to apprehend even as it is time to move on and transition to a state-of-the-art phase of your virtual nomad journey. In this subchapter, we are able to find out the signs and symptoms and symptoms that recommend it's time for a exchange and the way to navigate this transition successfully.

"Stop being frightened of what can also want to move

incorrect and reflect onconsideration on what may need to

pass proper."

One of the first signs and symptoms and signs and symptoms that it is able to be time to transition is a lack of concept or motivation on your modern-day location. As a virtual nomad, your environment plays a vital role on your productiveness and easy happiness.

If you locate your self feeling stagnant or uninspired for your modern-day holiday spot, it is able to be a signal that it's time to find out new horizons and are attempting to find smooth opinions.

Another indicator that it is time to transition is in case you've completed your desires to your cutting-edge place. Perhaps you got down to research a contemporary language or immerse yourself in a particular lifestyle, and you've were given finished the ones desires. Once you have ticked off the whole thing for your bucket list, it is herbal to start yearning new worrying situations and opportunities.

Financial concerns have to additionally be taken under consideration while finding out to transition. If you locate that the rate of residing in your present day area is becoming too burdensome or if you're suffering to hold your profits, it is able to be smart to maintain in mind transferring to a more less costly holiday spot or exploring new avenues for producing income.

Furthermore, private and professional relationships can substantially effect the selection to transition. If you've got shaped deep connections with locals or fellow digital nomads, leaving can be bittersweet. Similarly, when you have established a strong network that helps your paintings, it is crucial to assess the effect of leaving in your expert boom.

"We wander for distraction, however we

adventure for success."

Navigating the transition effectively calls for careful planning and schooling. Research functionality locations that align together collectively together with your goals and values.

Consider factors together with fee of dwelling, visa requirements, and hobby opportunities. Create a sturdy economic plan to make sure a smooth transition and function a backup plan in case matters do not flow as predicted.

Ultimately, recognizing whilst it's time to transition is an essential expertise for any digital nomad. By staying attuned to your desires, goals, and dreams, you can make well-knowledgeable choices so that it will hold to enhance your nomadic life-style. Embrace the uncertainty and include the following financial ruin of your virtual nomad journey with open hands.

"It doesn't rely in that you're

going, it's who you have have been given

beside you."

Preparing for the Repatriation

Process

As a digital nomad, the joys of residing and running in outstanding international locations can be an exquisite journey.

However, there may also furthermore come a time at the same time as making a decision to transport decrease back to your home u . S . A . Or loosen up in a contemporary region. This subchapter will guide you thru the technique of repatriation, helping you put together for a clean transition once more to your own home or a modern location.

1. Reflect on Your Experience: Before starting the repatriation technique, take some time to mirror to your experience as a virtual nomad. Think about what you have got located out, the demanding situations you've got triumph over, and the private growth you have got were given professional. This reflection will assist you understand how a while abroad has fashioned you and what you need to your destiny.

2. Evaluate Your Finances: Repatriating may be high-priced, so it's miles crucial to evaluate your price range and create a fee variety. Consider expenses like transportation,

transferring expenses, housing, and viable profession changes.

Start saving earlier to ensure a easy transition without any monetary strain.

3. Research the Job Market: If you intend to keep running remotely or in a current region, research the machine market in your home usa or the united states of a you desire to settle in. Explore capability job opportunities, networking sports, and organisation tendencies. By being properly-organized, you can hit the ground taking walks while you arrive.

4. Organize Your Documents: Repatriation frequently includes coping with numerous administrative responsibilities.

Make excessive excellent to build up and set up all the important files which encompass passports, visas, artwork lets in, and one-of-a-kind crook paperwork. Check the requirements for returning to your property u.S. Of the us or settling in a modern-day one to make certain a trouble-free system.

5. Connect with Your Network: Reach out for your expert and private community earlier than repatriating.

Inform them about your plans and unique your interest in pastime opportunities or connections in your preferred vicinity. Networking can play a crucial characteristic in finding employment or settling into a today's community.

6. Plan for Reverse Culture Shock: Reverse manner of life wonder is a common phenomenon skilled by way of manner of individuals returning to their home u.S.A. After an prolonged duration foreign places. Anticipate and prepare for ability demanding situations via using staying linked with friends and family, looking for help corporations, and attractive in sports that help you adjust on your new environment.

7. Embrace Change: Repatriation is a huge life alternate, and it is important to embody the manner with an open mind. Be organized for adjustments and be flexible in your expectancies. Use the abilties and studies gained at some stage in it gradual as a digital nomad to conform to new conditions and make the maximum of this thrilling transition.

The repatriation way can be every exciting and overwhelming. By following the ones steps and getting geared up yourself mentally, financially, and professionally, you may make sure a easy and a fulfillment transition lower lower back to your property u.S.A. Of the united states or a brand new location. Embrace the adjustments that lie earlier and maintain to conform as a digital nomad in a present day chapter of your existence.

"The reason is to die with memories

not desires"

Maintaining Relationships and

Connections

As a digital nomad, the capability to artwork and live everywhere within the international is each freeing and interesting.

However, this manner of life also can pose demanding situations with regards to preserving relationships and connections with cherished ones and associates again home. In this subchapter, we're capable to discuss some techniques and device that will help you live related and foster relationships whilst residing the digital nomad manner of life.

First and predominant, it's far essential to talk your intentions and plans for your family in advance than embarking on this journey. Explain why you've got decided in this way of life and the benefits it gives. By placing expectations and addressing any problems, you may maintain a robust basis on your relationships.

Chapter 10: Attractions Of Living A Nomadic Life

The nomadic life gives an not possible to withstand tapestry of points of hobby which have captivated hearts and minds throughout the globe. Escaping the monotony of ordinary, embracing cultural variety, and immersing oneself inside the ever-changing landscapes of the world are some of the primary allurements. The freedom to rouse to a dawn over an unexpected horizon, to sip espresso on a overseas balcony, and to stumble upon novel memories spherical each corner; the ones are the treasures that the nomadic way of life bestows. Beyond the enchantment of picturesque vistas, the nomadic lifestyles cultivate non-public growth, fostering a capability to navigate the uncharted waters of existence and profession.

Cultivating Flexibility and Adaptation Skills

At the coronary heart of the nomadic thoughts-set lies the know-how of pliability—an artwork form that allows one to thrive in the face of the unpredictable. Nomads turn out to be adept at adapting to new environments, unexpected traumatic conditions, and dynamic work settings. This flexibility extends beyond the professional realm; it shapes relationships, broadens perspectives, and instills a resilience that enriches every facet of lifestyles. As nomads learn how to navigate various time zones, languages, and cultural norms, they unveil a ordinary reality: that the capability to conform is the bedrock upon which the nomadic journey is constructed.

Conquering Fear and Embracing Change

Change can be daunting, and fear frequently serves as a barrier to getting into the unknown. The nomadic mindset, however, champions the art of conquering worry and embracing alternate as a catalyst for boom. By analyzing to stand uncertainty head-on, nomads cultivate a totally specific set of coping mechanisms that empower them to overcome demanding situations, every high-quality and small. The course of the nomad teaches that fear want no longer be a roadblock; alternatively, it could be a stepping stone inside the course of a life of profound transformation and unbounded capability.

As we embark in this exploration of the nomadic mind-set, we delve deeper into the mental panorama that underpins the digital nomad way of existence.

We will unveil private narratives of humans who've embraced this mind-set, reminiscences that display the inner workings in their hearts and minds as they navigate the complicated tapestry of trade, model, and discovery. In doing so, we release the secrets to no longer nice surviving but flourishing as modern-day nomads, geared up with the system to navigate the uncharted terrains of the digital desert.

In the location of virtual nomadism, the idea of the traditional office undergoes a exchange, transforming proper proper into a realm defined thru flexibility, adaptability, and innovation. As the current-day nomad navigates the ever-evolving landscape of remote art work, it turns into essential to put down a sturdy basis—a framework that helps seamless verbal exchange, enhances productiveness, and fosters a harmonious artwork-lifestyles aggregate. In this economic spoil, we delve into the critical components that represent this framework, exploring the craft of crafting an effective domestic workspace, the location of essential a ways flung paintings equipment and software utility, and the mastery of techniques for green time manipulate and productivity.

Crafting an Effective Home Workspace

The beauty of a long way flung art work lies in the freedom to mould one's environment to in shape character possibilities and desires. Crafting an effective domestic workspace, but, extends past the aesthetics—it's miles the art work of curating an surroundings that fosters cognizance, creativity, and comfort. Whether it is a sunlit corner overlooking a bustling street or a minimalist haven that encourages clarity of perception, the physical workspace turns into a canvas upon which productivity is painted.

We solve the nuances of ergonomics, business enterprise, and personalization that breathe life into a workspace, transforming it proper right into a sanctuary for innovation and accomplishment.

Indispensable Remote Work Tools and Software

In a global powered thru virtual marvels, the modern-day nomad's toolkit brims with an array of software application and gear that bridge distances and empower collaboration. From verbal exchange systems that move beyond time zones to mission control software program that maintains responsibilities on route, the ones digital companions weave a thread of connectivity via the nomad's journey. We delve into the landscape of essential equipment, exploring their functionalities, advantages, and the seamless integration that transforms them into integral allies in the realm of a ways flung artwork.

Techniques for Efficient Time Management and Productivity

As the nomadic voyage unfolds, the potential to manipulate time efficaciously and harness productiveness turns into paramount. Balancing the lure of exploration with the dreams of hard work calls for a touchy dance, one which desires field, attention, and a strategic method.

In this segment, we unveil an arsenal of techniques—starting from the Pomodoro technique to time-blockading techniques—that empower nomads to triumph over distractions, optimize art work hours, and domesticate a rhythm that harmonizes with their personal and professional aspirations.

As we traverse the panorama of crucial additives for some distance off artwork, we collect insights from seasoned nomads who have perfected the art work of an extended way flung productivity. Through their tales, we discover the threads that weave a tapestry of fulfillment—threads that remodel a trifling workspace into an oasis of innovation, that turn virtual equipment into catalysts for collaboration, and that infuse the adventure with the magic of powerful time control. Embracing this framework, the cutting-edge nomad embarks on a voyage empowered through generation and fueled through way of an unyielding willpower to excellence.

In the sector of digital nomadism, the area is your canvas, and every excursion spot is a stroke of color on the palette of your journey. From bustling metropolis landscapes to serene coastal retreats, the alternatives are as severa because the desires that fuel your nomadic aspirations. In this monetary disaster, we embark on a voyage of wanderlust, delving into the intricacies of choosing extraordinary nomad locations. We navigate the artwork of studying nomad-first-class places, get to the bottom of the delicate balance of allocating budget for fantastic locations, and manual you thru the maze of visa and crook worries that shape your route.

Researching Nomad-Friendly Places

The international is a tapestry of cultures, climates, and corporations, each imparting a very particular tapestry for the nomadic explorer. Yet, not all locations are created equal inside the eyes of the digital nomad. Researching nomad-great places involves more than virtually surfing through adventure brochures—it's approximately expertise the complicated dance amongst connectivity, charge of dwelling, and way of lifestyles alternatives. We delve into the elements that outline a haven for a long way flung paintings, from dependable internet infrastructure to a vibrant network of fellow nomads, assisting you find out locations that align seamlessly collectively together with your professional and private desires.

Allocating Finances for Different Locations

As you traverse the globe, your monetary panorama shifts, providing every opportunities and disturbing conditions. The cost of living, forex costs, and monetary situations range from one excursion spot to a few other, making financial making plans an critical element of your nomadic adventure. We guide you through the art work of allocating price range, supporting you strike a stability between experiencing the splendors of a ultra-modern way of life and maintaining economic stability. By gaining knowledge of the information of budgeting throughout diverse locations, you empower yourself to extract the most rate from every excursion spot on the equal time as safeguarding your lengthy-time period monetary health.

Navigating Visa and Legal Considerations

The nomadic trail intersects with a labyrinth of crook and visa troubles, each which includes a layer of complexity to your journey. Navigating the ones intricacies goals a eager information of immigration rules, paintings lets in, and visa options. From the mountains of office paintings to the functionality hurdles of get admission to, we demystify the approach, equipping you with the insights and assets to tread with a bit of excellent fortune via the legal panorama. By embracing an informed method to visa and legal concerns, you pave the way for a persevering with nomadic revel in, unburdened via bureaucratic limitations.

As we adventure via the bankruptcy, we weave memories of nomads who've traversed continents and crossed borders, every with a completely particular tale of discovery and variation. Through their critiques, you gain a firsthand attitude on the pains and triumphs of selecting fine nomad places. With each step, you discover the threads that bind geography, ambition, and adventure right into a persevering with tapestry, developing a roadmap in your very very own nomadic paradise.

In the nomadic realm, economic empowerment is the linchpin that transforms goals into fact and sustains the journey beforehand. As you embark on a lifestyles unconfined with the useful resource of borders, this financial disaster delves into the complex realm of handling finances, producing earnings on the flow, and navigating the intricacies of taxation and financial making plans throughout continents.

Chapter 11: Managing Finances And Budgeting As A Nomad

The nomadic way of life necessitates a fluid method to economic control, in which adaptability is as essential due to the truth the stability on your monetary organization account. This phase unravels the artwork of budgeting for the nomadic way of life—balancing the appeal of exploration with the obligation of economic balance. We find out strategies to tune fees, optimize spending, and domesticate a financial plan that empowers you to include the vicinity's wonders even as securing a valid economic destiny.

Approaches for Generating Income

In the digital age, the world becomes your marketplace, and your talents are your most precious overseas cash. This phase unveils a plethora of strategies to generating earnings while on the flow into.

From far flung freelancing and on-line groups to innovative ventures and digital entrepreneurship, you may find out a wealth of possibilities that empower you to monetize your passions and abilities, permitting you to hold your nomadic adventure while engaging in professional fulfillment.

Taxation and Financial Planning for Global Mobility

As a citizen of the place, the sector of taxation takes on a complicated and dynamic form. This section navigates the intricacies of taxation and economic planning for worldwide mobility, providing insights into the nuances of skip-border taxation, tax optimization strategies, and the significance of cultivating a strong monetary plan that aligns together collectively along with your nomadic aspirations. By harnessing a complete records of taxation, you empower your self to navigate the financial landscape with self assurance and maximize the rewards of your nomadic voyage.

As we traverse these chapters, you may weave a tapestry of monetary savvy and strategic desire-making, shaping a nomadic way of lifestyles that flourishes on empowerment, exploration, and monetary resilience. By embracing the paintings of excursion spot preference and economic empowerment, you embark on a adventure defined with the aid of boundless horizons and a liberated experience of possibility.

In the nomadic realm, life is a canvas painted with colourful strokes of exploration, journey, and private increase. Yet, amidst the exhilarating journey, lies the sensitive art of crafting a harmonious way of life that seamlessly blends art work, entertainment, and properly-being. This bankruptcy is a guide to accomplishing equilibrium in a lifestyles on the bypass—a adventure into the geographical areas of hard work-life balance, conquering solitude, and nurturing properly-being at the equal time as traversing the globe.

Striving for Work-Life Equilibrium whilst Traveling

The digital nomadic way of existence guarantees the freedom to pursue expert pursuits without sacrificing the delight of exploration. Balancing paintings and entertainment, but, calls for purpose and mindfulness. We delve into techniques for weaving artwork seamlessly into the fabric of your travels, nurturing a symbiotic relationship that lets in you to embody each productiveness and the splendor of the arena round you.

Tackling Loneliness and Isolation

While the nomadic adventure is a tapestry of pleasure, it is able to additionally unveil moments of solitude that check the spirit. This segment explores the art of tackling loneliness and isolation, guiding you through techniques to domesticate enormous connections with fellow vacationers and locals alike. From immersive cultural reminiscences to forging friendships in sudden corners of the area, you may discover a manner to transform moments of solitude into opportunities for profound boom and connection.

Prioritizing Wellness and Self-Care in the end of Travels

Amidst the excitement of new horizons lies the vital to prioritize your properly-being—a cornerstone of a sustainable nomadic manner of existence. This segment unravels the route to nurturing your physical, emotional, and intellectual nicely-being whilst on the go with the flow. From nicely being rituals that ground you in your adventure to self-care practices that foster resilience, you can embark on a transformative voyage of self-discovery, fueled via the belief that nurturing your self is crucial to crafting a harmonious and first-rate nomad way of life.

As a modern nomad, the region turns into your canvas, and connections with fellow tourists redecorate into brushstrokes that decorate your narrative. This monetary catastrophe delves into the essence of network and connection, guiding you thru the art work of identifying kindred spirits, embracing collaborative workspaces, and leveraging the strength of virtual networks to foster mutual assist.

Identifying and Engaging with Fellow Nomads

Amidst the large tapestry of worldwide exploration, the nomadic community serves as a compass, guiding you within the course of kindred spirits who share your ethos. This phase unveils techniques for identifying and tasty with fellow nomads, from sparking conversations in co-jogging regions to collaborating in nearby activities that unite like-minded individuals. By weaving those connections, you growth your horizons beyond geographical borders, forging friendships that boom your adventure.

Collaborative Workspaces and Networking Opportunities

The international itself will become your place of work, and collaborative workspaces offer a bridge among your professional interests and the landscapes that encourage you. This phase explores the dynamics of co-working regions—hubs of innovation and creativity that foster collaboration and connections with fellow nomads and close by entrepreneurs. Whether it's miles brainstorming intervals, ability-sharing, or serendipitous encounters, the ones regions end up crucibles of idea that fuel your nomadic venture.

Leveraging Virtual Communities for Mutual Support

The virtual age brings with it the electricity of virtual agencies—a web of connections that transcends borders and time zones. This segment delves into the world of on line boards, social media companies, and virtual networks that function lifelines for mutual assist. By tapping into the ones virtual avenues, you consist of a global tapestry of steerage, camaraderie, and shared information that enhances your nomadic adventure.

In the nomadic realm, the limits of profession dissolve, changed through a canvas of entrepreneurial possibilities and the autonomy to shape your private expert future. This financial ruin is a manual to launching your nomadic assignment—an exploration of constructing a a success freelance profession, transforming your passions into faraway business enterprise endeavors, and learning the art work of powerful marketing, branding, and consumer engagement.

Building a Successful Freelance Career Path

The nomadic way of life and freelancing move hand in hand, offering the liberty to take fee of your professional future. This phase delves into the artwork of building a a hit freelance profession course, guiding you thru the intricacies of finding clients, handling duties, and turning in extremely good rate at the equal time as at the flow into. By analyzing the nuances of freelancing, you unleash the capability to thrive to your phrases, embracing the rewards of flexibleness, independence, and achievement.

Transforming Passions into Remote Business Endeavors

The nomadic lifestyle is a canvas for creative entrepreneurship, allowing you to transform your passions into sustainable remote commercial organization ventures.

This section explores the journey of conceptualizing, launching, and scaling a business enterprise that aligns along side your know-how and passions. From e-change ventures to virtual merchandise, you may embark on a voyage of entrepreneurship that empowers you to harness your competencies and create a long lasting effect on a worldwide scale.

Strategies for Effective Marketing, Branding, and Client Engagement

In the digital landscape, effective marketing and branding are the motors that supply your message throughout continents. This segment unveils the strategies and techniques for crafting a compelling brand identity, correctly advertising your offerings, and tasty customers with authenticity and effect. By reading these factors, you domesticate a digital presence that resonates together with your audience, allowing you to forge lasting connections and create a thriving nomadic agency.

As we traverse those chapters, you'll embark on a adventure of stability, connection, and entrepreneurial increase—a voyage that empowers you to craft a harmonious way of life, installation extensive connections, and shape your professional future on a global degree. By embracing the nomadic way of lifestyles with cause and technique, you become the architect of a life that harmoniously blends exploration, reason, and success.

In the tapestry of the nomadic adventure, languages and cultures emerge as the great threads that weave through your evaluations.

This monetary catastrophe is a compass for navigating the rich style of the area—presenting insights into acquiring new languages, gracefully adapting to cultural shifts, and bridging gaps for significant pass-cultural verbal exchange.

Chapter 12: Navigating Cultural Shifts

As you traverse new horizons, languages turn out to be your key to unlocking deeper connections and immersing yourself in the tapestry of neighborhood cultures. This phase delves into the art work of obtaining new languages—a capacity that not excellent lets in conversation however moreover fosters a profound statistics of the locations you stumble upon. Alongside language acquisition, you can explore the location of cultural shifts—gracefully adapting to nearby customs, etiquette, and social norms to navigate the complicated maze of cultural range.

Respecting and Adapting to Local Traditions

Every nook of the world offers a tapestry of traditions and rituals, each a testomony to the uniqueness of the human revel in.

This section courses you through the art work of respecting and adapting to neighborhood traditions, making sure that your nomadic adventure is marked with the aid of the usage of sensitivity, cultural recognition, and a deep appreciation for the historical beyond of the locations you visit. By embracing local customs, you come to be a bridge amongst cultures, fostering connections that cross beyond language and geography.

Bridging Cultural Gaps for Enhanced Communication

Effective verbal exchange is the coronary heart beat of human connection, and within the nomadic realm, it will become a bridge that spans languages and cultures. This phase explores the nuances of float-cultural communication, equipping you with strategies to navigate language barriers, cultural nuances, and differing communication styles. By studying the art of bridging cultural gaps, you forge connections that circulate beyond linguistic obstacles, developing a symphony of data and shared reviews.

In the digital panorama that underpins the nomadic journey, generation becomes your steadfast partner—a conduit that connects you to the world and empowers your pursuits. This bankruptcy delves into the area of turning into a tech-savvy nomad, imparting insights into fine practices for cybersecurity, techniques for making sure connectivity, and a curated collection of critical apps and gadget that streamline your excursion making plans.

Optimal Practices for Cybersecurity in Remote Work

In a global described by using way of digital interactions, cybersecurity is an critical defend that safeguards your nomadic endeavors. This segment unravels the brilliant practices for preserving on-line protection, defensive touchy statistics, and navigating the digital landscape with self belief. By gaining knowledge of the art of cybersecurity, you empower yourself to artwork, speak, and find out with peace of mind, unfettered via manner of the usage of the danger of virtual vulnerabilities.

Ensuring Connectivity and Overcoming Digital Challenges

From bustling metropolises to a long way off corners of the arena, connectivity remains the lifeblood of the nomadic journey.

Essential Apps and Tools for Streamlined Travel Planning

In the current nomadic toolkit, apps and tools are your partners for streamlined tour making plans, inexperienced navigation, and greater appropriate exploration. This phase unveils a curated collection of vital apps and digital sources that empower you to plot your journeys with precision, discover hidden gem stones, and consist of the spontaneity that defines the nomadic manner of life. From language translation system to journey itinerary organizers, you may embark on a tech-infused journey that enhances each facet of your nomadic revel in.

Amidst the countless landscapes of the nomadic day adventure, locating refuge turns into a canvas for creativity and luxury. This bankruptcy is a guide to deciding on dwellings for short-term and lengthy-term remains, embracing co-residing preparations and house-sitting possibilities, and keeping a nurturing home base on the same time as traversing the globe.

Selecting Dwellings for Short-Term and Long-Term Stays

Every destination gives a spectrum of accommodations options, each contributing for your nomadic narrative. This section delves into the art of choosing dwellings for short-time period and prolonged-term remains, exploring the place of motels, hostels, Airbnb leases, and one-of-a-kind precise inns arrangements. By getting to know the nuances of accommodations choice, you create a haven that enriches your nomadic experience, imparting comfort, concept, and a experience of home in every nook of the world.

Co-dwelling Arrangements and House-Sitting Opportunities

In the nomadic landscape, co-residing and residence-sitting grow to be pathways to cultural immersion and connection.

This segment unveils the arena of co-dwelling arrangements—shared regions that foster collaboration, friendship, and go with the flow-cultural reviews. Alongside co-dwelling, you could explore the art work of residence-sitting—a completely unique opportunity to encompass community life at the same time as supplying a treasured company. By embracing these opportunity resorts solutions, you embark on a journey of enrichment and connection that transcends traditional resorts.

Chapter 13: Accessing Medical Services And Healthcare Abroad

In the large expanse of worldwide exploration, making sure your health and nicely-being transcends geographical boundaries. This section delves into the art work of gaining access to clinical offerings and healthcare remote places, offering insights into navigating remote places healthcare systems, looking for

scientific help, and embracing a proactive technique to nicely-being. By arming yourself with understanding, you empower your nomadic adventure with the guarantee of complete fitness care and safety.

Comprehensive Insight into Travel Insurance and Health Coverage for Nomads

As a vacationer unbound with the useful resource of borders, the arena of journey insurance and fitness insurance takes on paramount significance. This section gives a whole notion into the nuances of excursion coverage, equipping you with the system to choose out and personalize insurance that aligns together with your nomadic way of lifestyles. By reading the intricacies of coverage, you forge a protect of safety that ensures your fitness, monetary protection, and peace of thoughts as you embark for your worldwide odyssey.

Nurturing Physical Fitness and Mental Resilience eventually of Travels

Amidst the rhythm of your nomadic adventure, your physical and intellectual well-being become the muse of your resilience. This phase explores the paintings of nurturing physical health and mental nicely-being on the identical time as at the pass, supplying strategies to keep an active way of life, domesticate mindfulness, and navigate the emotional terrain of the nomadic way of life. By prioritizing holistic properly-being, you empower your self to thrive amidst the disturbing conditions and delights of your nomadic existence.

In the boundless expanse of exploration, the nomadic journey takes on an intrinsic responsibility—to leave a great imprint on the locations and groups you encounter. This financial ruin delves into the location of sustainability and aware nomadism, guiding you thru the art of minimizing ecological impact, contributing certainly to nearby cultures, and embracing green practices that enhance your nomadic way of existence.

Minimizing Ecological Impact via Responsible Travel

As a custodian of the Earth, your adventure incorporates a determination to treading lightly upon the landscapes you discover. This segment unveils the concepts of responsible journey, imparting techniques to lower your ecological footprint, defend fragile ecosystems, and depart inside the back of a legacy of recognize and stewardship. By embracing accountable adventure practices, you emerge as a father or mother of the planet, weaving sustainability into the very cloth of your nomadic life.

Contributing Positively to Local Communities and Cultures

The nomadic journey is a symphony of connections—among landscapes, cultures, and hearts. This phase delves into the artwork of contributing definitely to nearby organizations and cultures, providing insights into great interactions, ethical engagements, and projects that empower and uplift the places you visit. By fostering connections and leaving a first rate effect, you boom your nomadic narrative with reminiscences of giant exchanges and lasting contributions.

Embracing Eco-Friendly Practices for Enriching Nomadic Living

The nomadic lifestyle and eco-hobby converge in a tapestry of sustainable options and aware movements. This phase explores the vicinity of eco-friendly practices for enriching your nomadic way of lifestyles, from decreasing waste and preserving resources to embracing sustainable transportation and lodging alternatives. By aligning your alternatives together together with your values, you create a nomadic existence that harmonizes with the environment and resonates with the standards of stewardship and mindfulness.

In the arena of nomadic life, every step is an invite to delve into the splendor of the unknown, to embody the fun of journey, and to immerse your self within the wealthy tapestry of cultures that outline our worldwide. This financial break is a manual to sporting out experiential tour, embracing cultural exchanges, exploring herbal environments, and hanging a harmonious balance among paintings and exploration.

Engaging in Experiential Travel and Cultural Exchanges

The nomadic journey is an open invitation to immerse your self within the narratives of the arena—to have interaction with nearby cultures, have a laugh with proper testimonies, and forge connections that go beyond boundaries. This segment unveils the artwork of experiential excursion and cultural exchanges, guiding you via immersive sports activities activities, nearby traditions, and transformative encounters that increase your adventure and broaden your angle.

Exploring Natural Environments and Outdoor Pursuits

Nature turns into your playground in the nomadic tapestry, inviting you to discover pristine landscapes, consist of outdoor pursuits, and discover the awe-inspiring splendor of the arena.

This phase delves into the vicinity of exploring herbal environments, presenting insights into eco-adventures, out of doors sports activities, and responsible engagement with the wasteland. By venturing into the splendid out of doors, you awaken a feel of marvel and appreciation for the difficult wonders of the Earth.

Striking a Harmonious Balance Between Work and Exploration

In the nomadic symphony, work and exploration dance in concord, growing a rhythm that fuels your adventure. This section navigates the art of putting a harmonious balance among artwork and exploration, presenting techniques to optimize your productivity, embody spontaneity, and create a synergy between your expert aspirations and your thirst for adventure. By studying this touchy dance, you embark on a voyage that weaves productivity and exploration into a seamless narrative of success and increase.

As we traverse those chapters, you may embark on a holistic journey that encompasses health, sustainability, cultural immersion, and journey—a voyage that transforms you into a steward of nicely-being, a aware visitor, and an explorer of each the world and the self. By embracing those aspects of nomadic lifestyles, you craft a way of life that harmonizes with the planet, nurtures your soul, and infuses each step with motive and success.

In the nomadic voyage, annoying conditions and triumphs come to be the threads that weave a tapestry of resilience, growth, and accomplishment. This bankruptcy is a guide to navigating the usual obstacles encountered through virtual nomads, arming you with techniques to conquer setbacks, and illuminating the path towards non-public and expert triumphs. As you undertaking via the peaks and valleys of the nomadic landscape, you will discover the resilience that defines your journey and the celebrations that mark your milestones.

Typical Obstacles Encountered via Digital Nomads

The nomadic path isn't always with out its proportion of disturbing conditions—every a test of your resourcefulness, adaptability, and tenacity. This phase unveils the same old barriers encountered thru digital nomads, from logistical hurdles to moments of doubt and uncertainty. By knowledge those worrying conditions, you embark on a journey of preparedness, equipped to stand the complexities of the nomadic manner of life head-on.

Strategies for Overcoming Setbacks and Navigating Challenges

In the face of annoying situations, the nomadic spirit turns into a beacon of resilience, illuminating the direction beforehand. This segment gives strategies for overcoming setbacks, from cultivating a growth mind-set to trying to find steering from mentors and fellow nomads. By harnessing the ones device, you transform boundaries into stepping stones, navigating the labyrinth of challenges with grace and resolution.

Celebrating Personal and Professional Success Narratives

Amidst the tapestry of the nomadic narrative, triumphs stand as beacons of fulfillment and boom. This section is a celebration of personal and expert achievement narratives—tales of desires executed, dreams realized, and moments of pride that outline your nomadic odyssey. By embracing those narratives, you honor the milestones that enhance your journey and encourage fellow nomads to reach for his or her private aspirations.

As the chapters of your nomadic tale spread, the tapestry of your adventure turns into a testament to the spirit of exploration, resilience, and transformation. The epilogue is a second of mirrored image and projection—a place to contemplate the evolution of your nomadic path, form the chapters but to be written, and encourage others to embark on their non-public nomadic odyssey.

Reflections on the Nomadic Journey

In the stillness of mirrored photo, you trace the footprints of your nomadic passage—moments of marvel, demanding conditions surmounted, and the tapestry of connections that enrich your narrative. This phase offers a canvas for introspection, inviting you to contemplate the education decided out, the growth professional, and the profound effect of the nomadic manner of existence in your identification and worldview.

Shaping and Embracing the Future Nomadic Path

As the nomadic pioneer, you stand at the crossroads of opportunity—a steward of your personal future and a navigator of uncharted territories.

This section courses you in shaping and embracing the future nomadic path, presenting insights into placing new goals, increasing your horizons, and continuing the legacy of exploration and empowerment. By embracing the evolution of your adventure, you strong a vision that resonates collectively at the side of your aspirations and fuels the flame of perpetual discovery.

Inspiring Others to Embark on their Own Nomadic Odyssey

The pages of your nomadic tale emerge as an belief—a legacy that extends beyond non-public achievement to ignite the dreams of others. This section empowers you to encourage fellow tourists, guiding them in the path of the threshold of their very very very own nomadic odysseys. By sharing your reviews, insights, and triumphs, you turn out to be a beacon of opportunity, encouraging others to embody the nomadic spirit and embark on their very own transformative trips.

Chapter 14: Historical Evolution Of Remote Work

The roots of a long manner flung artwork can be traced again to the Nineteen Seventies while telecommuting end up first added. The concept turned into contemporary: with the advent of information generation, employees can also need to perform their obligations from home or a far flung area instead of commuting to an place of business. This early form of remote artwork modified into seen as a method to problems like net website visitors congestion, pollutants, and the need for a higher art work-existence stability.

As generation advanced, so did the possibilities for faraway art work? The internet and cloud computing made sharing and having access to facts a great deal less complex, taking part with agencies, and staying linked no matter geographical distances. By the early 2000s, the gig monetary gadget started out out to take form, with structures like Upwork and Fiverr allowing freelancers to paintings with clients from everywhere inside the worldwide.

Technology's Role in Enabling Remote Work

Technology has been the riding stress in the back of the rise of far off paintings. High-tempo internet connectivity, collaboration gear, and cloud-primarily based offerings have made it possible to art work successfully from anywhere. Video conferencing software like Zoom and collaboration platforms like Slack and Asana have enabled real-time conversation and assignment manipulate, breaking geographical barriers.

Impact of COVID-19 on Work Patterns

The COVID-19 pandemic had a profound effect on our artwork styles. With lockdowns and social distancing measures in location, companies global have been forced to adopt far off art work overnight. This speedy shift set up that many jobs may be performed remotely without significantly dropping productiveness.

The pandemic has also induced prolonged-term modifications in our artwork tradition. With the effectiveness of some distance off artwork validated many corporations within the mean time are presenting bendy paintings options or moving to a totally a long way flung version. Having expert the advantages of a long way flung art work, employees are trying to find jobs that provide flexibility and autonomy.

The Advantages and Disadvantages of Remote Work

Remote paintings offers numerous advantages, such as flexibility, price economic savings, and the functionality for a better artwork-lifestyles balance. It allows human beings to avoid demanding commutes, paintings in a cushty surroundings, and characteristic extra manage over their time.

However, some distance off art work moreover comes with disturbing conditions. These embody feelings of isolation, verbal exchange issues, and troubles in maintaining a clean boundary amongst art work and private lifestyles. It requires strength of will, sensible communication abilties, and adapting to a non-conventional paintings environment.

The Diversity of Remote Work: Different Industries and Roles

Remote artwork isn't always constrained to any enterprise or feature. Various industries offer a ways flung art work opportunities, from generation and advertising to education and healthcare. Roles that have been historically workplace-based totally completely are honestly being accomplished remotely, which include venture manage, customer support, and HR roles.

Emerging developments and possibilities in far off art work are constantly evolving. Virtual fact, AI, and blockchain are starting off new avenues for faraway paintings, developing roles that didn't exist a decade within the beyond. The future of far off work isn't always quite loads operating from domestic however about leveraging generation to paintings in new, modern-day-day strategies.

This historical perspective and expertise of far off work are crucial as we float inside the route of a destiny in which faraway artwork and virtual nomadism turns into the norm in vicinity of the exception.

Embracing the Digital Nomad Lifestyle

DEFINING THE DIGITAL NOMAD

The virtual nomad is a determine of the modern age a made from technological improvement, worldwide connectivity, and converting societal norms. But what exactly does it propose to be a virtual nomad?

At its center, a digital nomad utilises generation to perform their interest remotely and live a nomadic life-style. They are not tied down through way of bodily location, regularly opting to adventure and work from distinct locations across the arena. This way of life is made possible thru the proliferation of virtual device and excessive-pace net, allowing art work truly anywhere, from bustling metropolis espresso shops to tranquil beachside retreats.

Common Misconceptions

Despite the developing reputation of virtual nomadism, severa subjects even though need to be clarified about this manner of life. Some recollect it's a perpetual excursion, even as others view it as an escape from responsibilities. However, the fact is that being a digital nomad calls for area, resilience, and a bargain of annoying art work. It's no longer a extended excursion; it's a completely unique way of merging paintings with manner of existence options.

Benefits and Challenges of the Nomadic Lifestyle

The appeal of the virtual nomad life-style lies in its promise of freedom and versatility. The potential to discover new cultures, meet numerous people and enjoy the world at the equal time as retaining a profession is a fascinating prospect. It gives a way to interrupt unfastened from the nine-to-5 grind and the restrictions of a difficult and speedy place of business.

However, this manner of lifestyles moreover comes with its precise set of traumatic conditions. Instability may be a consistent companion with uncertain residing conditions, fluctuating profits, and the need to adapt to new environments commonly. Digital nomads often face cultural variations, language boundaries, and feelings of isolation. Plus, realistic issues like time vicinity versions, visa requirements, and making sure dependable net get admission to can upload to the complexity.

Real-life Stories: Case Studies of Successful Digital Nomads

Despite the ones traumatic conditions, countless human beings have efficiently embraced the digital nomad life-style, each with unique approaches and critiques.

For example, don't forget a settlement picture fashion fashion dressmaker who uses her capabilities to paintings with customers global on the identical time as exploring and drawing notion from the numerous cultures she immerses herself in. Or a software program developer who left his robust workplace way to excursion the world, going for walks with a disbursed group from awesome time zones.

Key training from their studies

These virtual nomads have faced annoying conditions, from finding reliable Wi-Fi in far off places to balancing the urge to discover with meeting art work time limits. Yet, they've located procedures to overcome those troubles, frequently mentioning that the benefits outweigh the issues.

From those recollections, key education emerge. Success as a virtual nomad regularly hinges on flexibility, resourcefulness, and paintings-life stability, even though those lines are blurred. It's approximately finding techniques to make art work complement your manner of life, no longer constrain it.

In scripting this, I apprehend it's important to keep in mind that reviews can range drastically, and what works for one person might not artwork for every other. Every digital nomad's adventure is particular, common thru their activities, career, and aspirations.

Preparing for Remote Work

SKILLS NECESSARY FOR REMOTE Work

In the world of far off paintings, some abilties maintain paramount importance. These can be divided into massive classes: technical and tender abilities. While technical abilties range depending at the undertaking's nature, particular easy competencies are universally beneficial for far off artwork.

Overview of Technical and Soft Skills

Technical abilities are the unique competencies needed to carry out a selected interest or undertaking. For instance, a photo style designer may need skillability in layout software program like Adobe Illustrator. In comparison, a much off customer support representative must use purchaser courting control (CRM) software program. Technical abilties frequently require formal schooling and education and are usually clean to quantify and evaluate.

On the opportunity hand, smooth abilities are extra subjective and harder to quantify. They relate to personal attributes and interpersonal competencies which could impact relationships, communication, and productivity within the place of business. For a long way flung employees, crucial smooth competencies encompass:

1. Communication Skills: Being a top notch communicator is vital in a much off paintings surroundings wherein groups are dispersed and direct; face-to-face interplay is restrained. This includes both written and verbal communication abilities.

2. Time Management: Remote art work regularly has bendy schedules, so you ought to control a while efficiently.

3. Self-Motivation: With the bodily presence of a fixed or supervisor, staying recommended can be easy. Remote humans ought to be self-starters who can maintain themselves on project.

four. Problem-Solving: Working remotely can supply precise challenges that want brief decision. Being able to hassle-solve and make options independently is critical.

5. Adaptability: Remote art work regularly requires coping with unexpected changes, including technical problems or schedule adjustments because of certainly one of a type time zones. Being adaptable allows some distance flung employees navigate the ones worrying situations efficaciously.

The Importance of Self-Motivation, Communication, and so forth.

In a miles off paintings environment, self-motivation and communique are specially important. Without the shape of a traditional workplace surroundings, it can be easy to lose interest or procrastinate. Self-motivation guarantees which you live green and meet your desires.

Communication is similarly important. As a much off worker, you'll depend cautiously on virtual communique system to live associated together along side your organization, communicate responsibilities, and replace your improvement. Being an powerful communicator will help save you misunderstandings, make certain anyone is on the same web page, and foster a revel in of teamwork, despite the fact that anybody is bodily aside.

That being said, at the same time as technical abilties are important in a long way off art work, smooth capabilities play an further, if not greater, significant position in figuring out your success as a miles flung worker. By developing those talents, you'll be nicely-equipped to thrive in a much flung paintings environment.

Please look at that the precise capabilities vital for faraway artwork can also range counting on the method characteristic and the specific paintings situations. It's essential to apprehend the requirements of your precise feature and constantly art work on growing your technical and smooth capabilities.

Online Courses and Resources for Skill Development

In the hastily evolving global of an extended way flung work and digital nomadism, staying earlier of the curve calls for non-prevent getting to know and know-how improvement. Fortunately, the digital landscape gives sufficient sources to beneficial useful resource your growth and make you a more powerful a long way off worker. Here are a few guidelines for applicable courses and schooling applications:

1. Digital Literacy and Productivity Tools:

Understanding and correctly the usage of virtual gadget is important for faraway paintings. Online systems like Coursera, Udemy, and LinkedIn Learning offer guides on digital literacy, which cowl important skills much like the use of Microsoft Office Suite, Google Workspace, and wonderful productiveness gear.

2. Project Management:

Remote paintings regularly consists of a couple of obligations or responsibilities. Platforms like Coursera and edX provide courses on venture manipulate, inclusive of methodologies like Agile and Scrum, which might be exceedingly valued in many a long way flung roles.

3. Communication:

Effective conversation is essential in a much flung art work placing. Business writing, public speaking, and interpersonal communication courses are supplied on Udemy and LinkedIn Learning.

4. Time Management and Productivity:

Staying effective in a miles flung work environment can be tough. Websites like Skillshare and MindTools provide sources and publications on time control, non-public productivity, and strain manage.

five. Technical Skills:

Depending in your area, you could want to increase particular technical abilties. Websites like Codecademy for coding, Adobe Creative Cloud for layout abilities, or DataCamp for facts evaluation provide enterprise-specific courses.

Chapter 15: Tips For Continuous Learning And Improvement

Continuous getting to know is a attitude; you may make it an enriching a part of your expert journey with the proper method. Here are a few recommendations:

1. Set Clear Goals: Identity which talents you want to amplify to excel on your faraway work feature. Having clean studying goals can manual your desire of guides and preserve you encouraged.

2. Make Learning a Routine: Dedicate regular time in your time table for analyzing. Spending half of-hour an afternoon on a path or reading up on business enterprise trends can yield noteworthy outcomes over the years.

3. Apply What You Learn: Implement what you study to your paintings proper now. This reinforces your new information and lets in you to peer its practical blessings.

4. Stay Curious: The worldwide of far off artwork is commonly evolving, and new equipment and practices are often rising. Stay open and curious about those modifications, and don't hesitate to research a few component new, regardless of the fact that it's outdoor your consolation region.

five. Join Online Communities: Engage with on line communities related to your field or an extended manner off artwork. These agencies may be first-rate property for getting to know, sharing expertise, and staying up to date on enterprise dispositions.

Leveraging on-line courses and fostering a non-stop studying mind-set guarantees you're nicely-ready to thrive in some distance flung artwork.

Building an Effective CV for Remote Work

Crafting a CV for a much off function calls for more than just list your skills and opinions. It's approximately demonstrating your capability to excel in a far off paintings surroundings.

Here are some hints on a way to tailor your CV to consciousness for your remote paintings competencies and stand out inside the competitive project marketplace:

1. Highlight Your Remote Work Experience:

If you've had any preceding experience walking remotely, make sure to spotlight it on your CV. This could be complete-time far flung roles, freelance paintings, or intervals while you worked from home in a traditional task. Don't absolutely list the jobs; provide records for your obligations, the machine you used, and the effects you performed. This will display functionality employers that you may be efficient and powerful remotely.

2. Emphasise Your Self-Motivation and Discipline:

Remote paintings requires a excessive degree of self-motivation and subject. Use your CV to expose examples of responsibilities or responsibilities in which you've confirmed those tendencies. Whether it's a challenge you completed beforehand of time table, a trouble you solved independently, or a aim you finished through regular effort, the ones examples will display your capability to live targeted and effective with out consistent supervision.

three. Showcase Your Communication Skills:

Effective verbal exchange is vital in a far off paintings putting. Highlight any studies demonstrating your capability to speak well, mainly in writing. This may be something from authoring reviews, developing displays, or handling a business organization company blog. If you've had experience with communication gadget like Slack, Zoom, or Microsoft Teams, factor out them.

four. Demonstrate Your Technological Proficiency:

Working remotely frequently includes the use of numerous digital device and systems. List the device you're familiar with, which embody venture manage software program (e.G., Asana, Trello), file-sharing platforms (e.G., Google Drive, Dropbox), or any industry-unique software. If you've ever educated others to apply the ones gadget or placed some aspect new, point out this to show your ability to conform to new generation.

five. Include Relevant Soft Skills:

Specific smooth abilties are specially precious in a miles off artwork putting. Employers hiring for an extended manner flung positions in particular are on the lookout for abilties like time control, adaptability, proactive trouble-fixing, and the ability to artwork independently. Use unique examples to reveal how you've used those talents for your artwork experience.

6. Tailor Your CV to Each Job:

Finally, hold in thoughts to tailor your CV to every hobby you exercise for. Carefully have a study the gadget description and wholesome your abilities and revel in to the requirements. Use their language to provide an explanation for your abilties and evaluations. This suggests employers which you've taken the time to apprehend the feature and its requirements, and it could moreover help your CV get beyond applicant monitoring systems.

A nicely-crafted CV may be the important thing to landing your excellent faraway venture. Take the time to recognition on your capabilities, testimonies, and accomplishments that show you could thrive in a much off artwork surroundings. With some attempt to approach, you can stand out within the competitive a ways flung hobby marketplace and constant a role that gives you the ability and freedom you're trying to find.

Showcasing Remote Work Skills

As faraway paintings will become increasingly more traditional, highlighting your functionality to art work effectively in a miles flung surroundings is important. Here are some guidelines on a manner to perform that:

1. Highlight Relevant Skills in Your CV: Include applicable talents for some distance flung art work. These include talent with a long way off paintings equipment, time manipulate, self-motivation, digital verbal exchange, and hassle-solving.

2. Showcase Past Remote Work Experience: If you've got formerly labored remotely, even for a fast length, make certain to focus on this experience. Specify your duties, the equipment you used, and the consequences you done.

three. Demonstrate Soft Skills: Soft competencies are important to a success a ways flung paintings. Skills like adaptability, power of thoughts, and effective communique are quite valued. Provide examples of methods you've used those abilties in beyond roles.

four. Include Certifications or Courses: If you've completed any publications or certifications applicable to a ways flung art work, along with virtual communique or mission management courses, include those in your CV.

Standing Out in the Remote Job Market

The an extended manner off project marketplace may be competitive, so it's crucial to distinguish yourself from other applicants. Here are some techniques to help you stand out:

1. Tailor Your Application: Make advantageous your CV and cowl letter are tailor-made to each activity you exercise for. Highlight the talents and studies that make you a sturdy healthful for the feature.

2. Build an Online Presence: A sturdy on line presence let you stand out. This may be a professional net website online, blog, or LinkedIn profile that suggests your talents, portfolio, and expert achievements.

3. Network: Networking remains vital within the faraway task market. Attend virtual business enterprise occasions, participate in relevant on line companies, and hook up with specialists for your area.

4. Show Enthusiasm for Remote Work: Employers need to recognise that you may enjoy an extended way off paintings. Express your enthusiasm for far flung paintings for your software and interview.

5. Follow-Up: Remember to follow up after filing your software program. A quick, well mannered electronic mail reiterating your hobby inside the feature will let you live pinnacle of mind.

With the ones techniques, you may effectively spotlight your far flung art work talents and stand out inside the an extended way off approach market.

www.ingramcontent.com/pod-product-compliance
Lightning Source LLC
Chambersburg PA
CBHW071440080526
44587CB00014B/1936